TED HUGHES Poems selected by SIMON ARMITAGE

D1366249

TED HUGHES
Poems selected by
SIMON ARMITAGE

ff

faber and faber

First published in 2000
by Faber and Faber Limited
3 Queen Square London WC1N 3AU

Photoset by Parker Typesetting Service, Leicester
Printed in Italy

All rights reserved

Introduction and selection © Simon Armitage, 2000
Poems © The Estate of Ted Hughes, 1995, 1997

Simon Armitage is hereby identified as editor of
this work in accordance with Section 77
of the Copyright, Designs and Patents Act 1988

*This book is sold subject to the condition that it shall not,
by way of trade or otherwise, be lent, resold, hired out or
otherwise circulated without the publisher's prior consent in
any form of binding or cover other than that in which it is
published and without a similar condition including this
condition being imposed on the subsequent purchaser*

A CIP record for this book
is available from the British Library
ISBN 0–571–20363–9

L134, 835 ANF 821 /914

10 9 8 7 6 5 4 3 2 1

Contents

Introduction

Putting together and publishing a selection of Ted Hughes's poetry today is a very different task than it would have been twenty years ago. When Hughes died in 1998, he was as valued and admired as at any time in his career, and his two final collections, *Tales from Ovid* and *Birthday Letters*, had met with resounding acclaim. In that respect alone, the task of assembling this book comes with all sorts of extra frisson and significance.

During the seventies and eighties, however, to speak up on behalf of Hughes, whether as a reader or writer, was to take a position. To support Hughes's poetry was to support the man himself, a man whose ideologies could have been described as unfashionable, and whose poetic style was seen by some as stubborn and entrenched. Hughes himself had become increasingly private and his poetry seemed to be in hiding with him. The criticisms over his role in the death of his first wife, Sylvia Plath, had reached fever pitch, especially in the United States, and even those with little or no knowledge of his poetry were quick to offer an opinion of it. For many, he represented the antithesis of contemporary ideology and modern political thought. His acceptance of the Laureateship in 1984 and his well-documented interest in hunting, shooting and fishing were easily caricatured. In that era, to be seen promoting the work of the man could have been construed as an act of defiance almost, rather than the act of celebration it is today. How quickly and how strangely situations turn about.

Possibly the tide will turn again, but Hughes's poetry has reached a new high-water mark in recent years. *Birthday Letters* is now one of the biggest-selling poetry titles of all time, with sales climbing towards the half-a-million mark. Its readership might well include a substantial number of ghouls, voyeurs and gossips with a less than literary interest in

Hughes's candid descriptions of his relationship with Plath – the white heat of their time together and her subsequent suicide – and the book also contains details of a second relationship which ended in still greater tragedy. But it is the quality of the writing that brought *Birthday Letters* such recognition, a quality of extraordinariness that for many of Hughes's supporters has been present throughout. It is worth noting that aside from the steady, sometimes obligatory admiration of his contemporaries, interest in Hughes's work has been renewed and revitalized by a younger generation of writers, many of whom have talked about the importance and influence of his poetry. The swag-bag of prizes and plaudits that Hughes carried off for those last two publications – pretty much a clean sweep of the board in the case of *Birthday Letters* – owed much to a new wave of poets, keen to make public an affiliation they had felt for years. It was a case of poets having their say, poetry putting its own house in order. Once that had happened, the ingrained polarity of the media seemed to reverse overnight, and suddenly it was acceptable for ordinary people to be seen in public places reading a book of poetry – and one written by Ted Hughes at that.

But if editing this volume is a thrill, there is also a sense of trepidation and responsibility associated with the project. Throughout his life, Hughes practised (quite rightly) a strict control over his work, being extremely careful as to its context, its presentation, and its timing. Poems were kept on a tight leash, invitations to read were very often declined, launch-dates were calculated by means of star-charts and zodiacal coincidences. For a writer of Hughes's stature, there are surprisingly few critical books on the market; those which do exist are engrossing and distinctive, for the main part, but have not come from the usual sources or been written by the usual suspects. (The number of available discourses on Plath makes an interesting comparison.) With Hughes no longer around to shepherd his poetry, that situation will surely change, and no doubt his death-knell will sound to some like a starting-pistol, triggering several unauthorized biographies. Some may be with us sooner than we like; biographers, like obituary writers, have a tendency to jump the gun, and don't always wait for the death before getting stuck into the life. We can only hope that any such books do proper justice to their subject.

Perhaps there has been a sense, within the world of writing and further afield, that Ted Hughes was not a man to be messed with, and therefore that his poetry wasn't something to be messed with either. It is an image at odds with the supportive, generous and enigmatic person that many found him to be, but an image that persisted nevertheless, possibly as an extension of his subject matter and poetic style. As far as I am aware, there are no previous selections of his work in which Hughes didn't have either complete control or at least a meaningful, supervisory presence, a presence which I still feel, and one that I need to respect. Hughes's *New Selected Poems* was published just three years before his death. Some writers, in their later life, have attempted a kind of self-revisionism that borders on the insane, making final, definitive selections of their work that have mystified and antagonized scholars and readers. Hughes, however, was as sharp as ever and possibly at his shrewdest during his later years, as the timing of *Birthday Letters* demonstrates, and there is every reason to trust in the final judgement he made concerning the poems he believed to be most successful. It is not the purpose of this volume to revise that judgement, but simply to further refine it into a more concentrated form, and to add a small amount of catalytic material into the equation. Ideally, I would have liked to have included pieces from some of Hughes's theatre works, and at least one short story, probably 'The Deadfall'. But for the moment there is a greater pressure to concentrate on the poems, and hopefully readers will be persuaded to investigate other dimensions of his work, just as Hughes himself investigated the boundaries of his talent through explorations into drama and prose.

Even when out of favour with the opinion-makers, Hughes still attracted the kind of attention that most poets would kill for, and every move he made was guaranteed a certain amount of notice, from serious reviews of his books, to journalists standing on the graveyard wall adjoining his house to take photographs through the windows. In fact, right from the appearance of his first book, *The Hawk in the Rain*, he was famous. Hughes was onto something that set him apart from his contemporaries. His concerns with animal instincts, ancient lore and the manifestations of nature were at variance with the sociological preoccupation of fellow poets, and his language – a sort of agricultural dialect of the Bible – was a far cry from the up-to-the-minute vocabularies of his peers. His interest in European poetry was undoubtedly helpful in the shaping and development of his voice, especially in *Crow*, where Hughes was at his most robust, uncompromising and apocalyptic.

Interestingly, though, and despite the complex philosophical subjects of his work, it was in the classrooms of Britain where Hughes's poetry found much of its loyal audience. My own experience as an uninspired and uninspiring secondary school student is one shared by many of the same age group, in the way that Hughes's poems were the first captivating moments in English literature, and were read and described by teachers who could not hide their enthusiasm for the work or their eagerness to share it. Poems like 'Wind', 'The Bull Moses', 'The Horses' and of course 'Hawk Roosting' are not only fastened in the imagination of a whole generation, but for some, like myself, were a kind of Rosetta Stone – the means by which the surrounding world could suddenly be translated, understood, and experienced. It is a particular virtue of Hughes's poetry, and one that he shares with only the very best poets, that clarity and complexity can exist simultaneously, like clear, still water, into which a person can see to a ponderous depth. No one could ever accuse Hughes of simplicity or superficiality, and yet his poems have an immediacy that students, even of a young age, find alluring and true. They draw the reader in, like black holes, whose event-horizons are instant, but whose intensities are infinite and utterly absorbing. His Noah-like cataloguing of the animal kingdom is of course a further lure to younger readers. Hughes was a determined educationalist; his book *Poetry in the Making*, taken from programmes written for the Schools' Broadcasting Department, is a valuable text for poets of any age, would-be or established, and his books for children represent a sizeable proportion of his output. As a follower of his work, I find it impossible not to see this as strategic, rather than accidental or sentimental, and part of Hughes's ambition to enter the world of intuition, innocence, and possibility.

I have come a long way in this introduction without, except for the scattering of adjectives, describing the work. Possibly the poems speak for themselves by now and need no further explanation, possibly an overview of Hughes's writing through his dozens of books is beyond the scope of this commentary, or possibly the detailing of poetic intent and achievement can only lead to a narrowing of interpretation rather than the ever-expanding experience that poetry should provide. In any case, such is the range of Hughes's poetry that a partial synopsis would not serve it well. His profound interest in history and prehistory, his arguments as to the monarchistic structure of the human imagination, his take on nature, his almost obsessional fixation with the First World War, his observations as to the sexual-courtship practised by poets through their work, are just a few of the interwoven and tangled threads. They need teasing out carefully, with due process.

But one theme which is worth enlarging on is the issue of Hughes's fascination with the supernatural and the para-normal. From an early age, Hughes demonstrated an uncommon interest in all things other-worldly, an interest furthered by his choice of studies at university and his background reading. Anyone who spent any time with him will have experienced this at first hand; his conversations were full of the weird and wonderful, from poltergeists to pixies, from witchcraft to ouija boards, from astrology to apparitions, from dousing to divination, and so on. It would be easy to pass this off as so much hocus-pocus, serving no literary purpose other than providing reams of subject-matter and bumping up the poet's credentials as a latter-day witch-doctor. But Hughes wasn't someone who pursued interests casually or without reason, and his dabblings in the occult were, to him, nothing less than an essential part of his task. Hughes aligned himself with the ancient role of the poet. He looked even further than the metaphysical potential of poetry to a kind of writing that had the power to heal and transform, to change perceptions and to alter states. He saw beyond the power to communicate, aiming instead for a kind of 'contact', or sensual comprehension, where poem and reader took possession of each other through the medium of poetry, or through the poet as medium. And he saw language as one of the least understood powers in the universe, ranking along-side electrical, gravitational, atomic and magnetic energy as a force to be manipulated and controlled. His view of the poet as shaman was one he took seriously, and many of his poems are unembarrassed shamanic flights of fancy into the spirit-world, excursions to the 'other side', where he might properly inhabit the nature of his subject, be it animal, vegetable or mineral, be it jaguar, snowdrop or rocky crag. He had a clear vision of his duties, and one of those duties was to convince his audience. Hughes was well aware of the potency and authority of his speaking voice, not to mention his personality, and put these attributes to good use. It was all part of the job. People had to believe in him. The word magic these days might conjure up images of a man pulling rabbits from a top hat or producing cards from under his cuffs. But Hughes's magic was his writing. He made little black marks against clean white pages, marks that somehow detailed the absolute matter and manner of a bird or an eel or a foal or a wolf or a bear. At later dates and in distant locations, when we looked at those marks, when we read the poems, those creatures came to life. Out of nothing. Has any other magician ever pulled off a greater trick?

Hughes, for me, was the man from over the top of the hill, from the next Yorkshire valley, and his poems made me want to read. Later, it was homesickness that drew me back to his work, and by that time his poems were making me want to write. I think we shared a nostalgia for the same part of the world, even if that patch of the planet held a different significance for us.

The first time I saw him was on a school English trip to Hebden Bridge, where he read his poems in a moth-eaten cinema, sitting on a creaking wooden chair in front of a threadbare velvet curtain. Over the next twenty years I met him about a dozen times, in some very obscure circumstances and peculiar company. We had certain common interests, but our meetings were always lopsided, by definition, because one of my interests was him. On the last occasion, I sat and listened as he made his last recorded reading, the poems from *Tales from Ovid* that were taped at his home and broadcast on BBC Radio 4. Hughes lowered his head to the microphone, and like the storyteller he truly was, told the whole story, beginning to end, with barely a fluff. Those cassettes are now available to all, but for all their slick packaging and promotion, they have for me the quality of a rare bootleg. Anyone listening carefully will be able to hear not just Hughes's voice at its ghostly, intimate best, but also the sounds of the Devon landscape going on around him. At one point there's a tractor. A little later, church bells. And eventually, right on cue, a crow comes winging its way through the stereo, in one ear and out through the other. It's a compelling testament to the work of a poet whose great exploit was to bring the inner workings of the human brain out into the wide world, and at the same time draw the outside world into the mind.

Simon Armitage

TED HUGHES

The Thought-Fox

I imagine this midnight moment's forest:
Something else is alive
Beside the clock's loneliness
And this blank page where my fingers move.

Through the window I see no star:
Something more near
Though deeper within darkness
Is entering the loneliness:

Cold, delicately as the dark snow
A fox's nose touches twig, leaf;
Two eyes serve a movement, that now
And again now, and now, and now

Sets neat prints into the snow
Between trees, and warily a lame
Shadow lags by stump and in hollow
Of a body that is bold to come

Across clearings, an eye,
A widening deepening greenness,
Brilliantly, concentratedly,
Coming about its own business

Till, with a sudden sharp hot stink of fox
It enters the dark hole of the head.
The window is starless still; the clock ticks,
The page is printed.

The Jaguar

The apes yawn and adore their fleas in the sun.
The parrots shriek as if they were on fire, or strut
Like cheap tarts to attract the stroller with the nut.
Fatigued with indolence, tiger and lion

Lie still as the sun. The boa-constrictor's coil
Is a fossil. Cage after cage seems empty, or
Stinks of sleepers from the breathing straw.
It might be painted on a nursery wall.

But who runs like the rest past these arrives
At a cage where the crowd stands, stares, mesmerized,
As a child at a dream, at a jaguar hurrying enraged
Through prison darkness after the drills of his eyes

On a short fierce fuse. Not in boredom –
The eye satisfied to be blind in fire,
By the bang of blood in the brain deaf the ear –
He spins from the bars, but there's no cage to him

More than to the visionary his cell:
His stride is wildernesses of freedom:
The world rolls under the long thrust of his heel.
Over the cage floor the horizons come.

Famous Poet

Stare at the monster: remark
How difficult it is to define just what
Amounts to monstrosity in that
Very ordinary appearance. Neither thin nor fat,
Hair between light and dark,

And the general air
Of an apprentice – say, an apprentice house-
Painter amid an assembly of famous
Architects: the demeanour is of mouse,
Yet is he monster.

First scrutinize those eyes
For the spark, the effulgence: nothing. Nothing there
But the haggard stony exhaustion of a near-
Finished variety artist. He slumps in his chair
Like a badly hurt man, half life-size.

Is it his dreg-boozed inner demon
Still tankarding from tissue and follicle
The vital fire, the spirit electrical
That puts the gloss on a normal hearty male?
Or is it women?

The truth – bring it on
With black drapery, drums and funeral tread
Like a great man's coffin – no, no, he is not dead
But in this truth surely half-buried:
Once, the humiliation

Of youth and obscurity,
The autoclave of heady ambition trapped,
The fermenting of the yeasty heart stopped –
Burst with such pyrotechnics the dull world gaped
And 'Repeat that!' still they cry.

But all his efforts to concoct
The old heroic bang from their money and praise
From the parent's pointing finger and the child's amaze,
Even from the burning of his wreathed bays,
　　Have left him wrecked: wrecked,

　　And monstrous, so,
As a Stegosaurus, a lumbering obsolete
Arsenal of gigantic horn and plate
From a time when half the world still burned, set
　　To blink behind bars at the zoo.

The Horses

I climbed through woods in the hour-before-dawn dark.
Evil air, a frost-making stillness,

Not a leaf, not a bird, –
A world cast in frost. I came out above the wood

Where my breath left tortuous statues in the iron light.
But the valleys were draining the darkness

Till the moorline – blackening dregs of the brightening
   grey –
Halved the sky ahead. And I saw the horses:

Huge in the dense grey – ten together –
Megalith-still. They breathed, making no move,

With draped manes and tilted hind-hooves,
Making no sound.

I passed: not one snorted or jerked its head.
Grey silent fragments

Of a grey silent world.

I listened in emptiness on the moor-ridge.
The curlew's tear turned its edge on the silence.

Slowly detail leafed from the darkness. Then the sun
Orange, red, red erupted.

Silently, and splitting to its core tore and flung cloud,
Shook the gulf open, showed blue,

And the big planets hanging –
I turned

Stumbling in the fever of a dream, down towards
The dark woods, from the kindling tops,

And came to the horses.
                              There, still they stood,
But now steaming and glistening under the flow of light,

Their draped stone manes, their tilted hind-hooves
Stirring under a thaw while all around them

The frost showed its fires. But still they made no sound.
Not one snorted or stamped,

Their hung heads patient as the horizons
High over valleys, in the red levelling rays –

In din of the crowded streets, going among the years, the
    faces,
May I still meet my memory in so lonely a place

Between the streams and the red clouds, hearing curlews,
Hearing the horizons endure.

KU-625-548

Wind

This house has been far out at sea all night,
The woods crashing through darkness, the booming hills,
Winds stampeding the fields under the window
Floundering black astride and blinding wet

Till day rose; then under an orange sky
The hills had new places, and wind wielded
Blade-light, luminous black and emerald,
Flexing like the lens of a mad eye.

At noon I scaled along the house-side as far as
The coal-house door. Once I looked up –
Through the brunt wind that dented the balls of my eyes
The tent of the hills drummed and strained its guyrope,

The fields quivering, the skyline a grimace,
At any second to bang and vanish with a flap:
The wind flung a magpie away and a black-
Back gull bent like an iron bar slowly. The house

Rang like some fine green goblet in the note
That any second would shatter it. Now deep
In chairs, in front of the great fire, we grip
Our hearts and cannot entertain book, thought,

Or each other. We watch the fire blazing,
And feel the roots of the house move, but sit on,
Seeing the window tremble to come in,
Hearing the stones cry out under the horizons.

October Dawn

October is marigold, and yet
A glass half full of wine left out

To the dark heaven all night, by dawn
Has dreamed a premonition

Of ice across its eye as if
The ice-age had begun its heave.

The lawn overtrodden and strewn
From the night before, and the whistling green

Shrubbery are doomed. Ice
Has got its spearhead into place.

First a skin, delicately here
Restraining a ripple from the air;

Soon plate and rivet on pond and brook;
Then tons of chain and massive lock

To hold rivers. Then, sound by sight
Will Mammoth and Sabre-tooth celebrate

Reunion while a fist of cold
Squeezes the fire at the core of the world,

Squeezes the fire at the core of the heart,
And now it is about to start.

Bayonet Charge

Suddenly he awoke and was running – raw
In raw-seamed hot khaki, his sweat heavy,
Stumbling across a field of clods towards a green hedge
That dazzled with rifle fire, hearing
Bullets smacking the belly out of the air –
He lugged a rifle numb as a smashed arm;
The patriotic tear that had brimmed in his eye
Sweating like molten iron from the centre of his chest –

In bewilderment then he almost stopped –
In what cold clockwork of the stars and the nations
Was he the hand pointing that second? He was running
Like a man who has jumped up in the dark and runs
Listening between his footfalls for the reason
Of his still running, and his foot hung like
Statuary in mid-stride. Then the shot-slashed furrows

Threw up a yellow hare that rolled like a flame
And crawled in a threshing circle, its mouth wide
Open silent, its eyes standing out.
He plunged past with his bayonet towards the green hedge,
King, honour, human dignity, etcetera
Dropped like luxuries in a yelling alarm
To get out of that blue crackling air
His terror's touchy dynamite.

Mayday on Holderness

This evening, motherly summer moves in the pond.
I look down into the decomposition of leaves –
The furnace door whirling with larvae.

        From Hull's sunset smudge
Humber is melting eastward, my south skyline:
A loaded single vein, it drains
The effort of the inert North – Sheffield's ores.
Bog pools, dregs of toadstools, tributary
Graves, dunghills, kitchens, hospitals.
The unkillable North Sea swallows it all.
Insects, drunken, drop out of the air.

            Birth-soils,
The sea-salts, scoured me, cortex and intestine,
To receive these remains.
As the incinerator, as the sun,
As the spider, I had a whole world in my hands.
Flowerlike, I loved nothing.
Dead and unborn are in God comfortable.
What a length of gut is growing and breathing –
This mute eater, biting through the mind's
Nursery floor, with eel and hyena and vulture,
With creepy-crawly and the root,
With the sea-worm, entering its birthright.

The stars make pietas. The owl announces its sanity.

The crow sleeps glutted and the stoat begins.
There are eye-guarded eggs in these hedgerows,
Hot haynests under the roots in burrows.
Couples at their pursuits are laughing in the lanes.

The North Sea lies soundless. Beneath it
Smoulder the wars: to heart-beats, bomb, bayonet.

'Mother, Mother!' cries the pierced helmet.
Cordite oozings of Gallipoli,

Curded to beastings, broached my palate,
The expressionless gaze of the leopard,
The coils of the sleeping anaconda,
The nightlong frenzy of shrews.

February

The wolf with its belly stitched full of big pebbles;
Nibelung wolves barbed like black pineforest
Against a red sky, over blue snow; or that long grin
Above the tucked coverlet – none suffice.

A photograph: the hairless, knuckled feet
Of the last wolf killed in Britain spoiled him for wolves:
The worst since has been so much mere Alsatian.
Now it is the dream cries 'Wolf!' where these feet

Print the moonlit doorstep, or run and run
Through the hush of parkland, bodiless, headless;
With small seeming of inconvenience
By day, too, pursue, siege all thought;

Bring him to an abrupt poring stop
Over engravings of gibbet-hung wolves,
As at a cage where the scraggy Spanish wolf
Danced, smiling, brown eyes doggily begging

A ball to be thrown. These feet, deprived,
Disdaining all that are caged, or storied, or pictured,
Through and throughout the true world search
For their vanished head, for the world

Vanished with the head, the teeth, the quick eyes –
Now, lest they choose his head,
Under severe moons he sits making
Wolf-masks, mouths clamped well onto the world.

Dick Straightup

Past eighty, but never in eighty years –
Eighty winters on the windy ridge
Of England – has he buttoned his shirt or his jacket.
He sits in the bar-room seat he has been
Polishing with his backside sixty-odd years
Where nobody else sits. White is his head,
But his cheek high, hale as when he emptied
Every Saturday the twelve-pint tankard at a tilt,
Swallowed the whole serving of thirty eggs,
And banged the big bass drum for Heptonstall –
With a hundred other great works, still talked of.
Age has stiffened him, but not dazed or bent,
The blue eye has come clear of time:
At a single pint, now, his memory sips slowly,
His belly strong as a tree bole.

He survives among hills, nourished by stone and height.
The dust of Achilles and Cuchulain
Itches in the palms of scholars; thin clerks exercise
In their bed-sitters at midnight, and the meat salesman can
Loft fully four hundred pounds. But this one,
With no more application than sitting,
And drinking, and singing, fell in the sleet, late,
Dammed the pouring gutter; and slept there; and,
    throughout
A night searched by shouts and lamps, froze,
Grew to the road with welts of ice. He was chipped out at
    dawn
Warm as a pie and snoring.

The gossip of men younger by forty years –
Loud in his company since he no longer says much –
Empties, refills and empties their glasses.
Or their strenuous silence places the dominoes

(That are old as the house) into patterns
Gone with the game; the darts that glint to the dartboard
Pin no remarkable instant. The young men sitting
Taste their beer as by imitation,
Borrow their words as by impertinence
Because he sits there so full of legend and life
Quiet as a man alone.

He lives with sixty and seventy years ago,
And of everything he knows three quarters is in the grave,
Or tumbled down, or vanished. To be understood
His words must tug up the bottom-most stones of this
    village,
This clutter of blackstone gulleys, peeping curtains,
And a graveyard bigger and deeper than the village
That sways in the tide of wind and rain some fifty
Miles off the Irish sea.
                    The lamp above the pub-door
Wept yellow when he went out and the street
Of spinning darkness roared like a machine
As the wind applied itself. His upright walk,
His strong back, I commemorate now,
And his white blown head going out between a sky and an
    earth
That were bundled into placeless blackness, the one
Company of his mind.

Obit

Now, you are strong as the earth you have entered.

This is a birthplace picture. Green into blue
The hills run deep and limpid. The weasel's
Berry-eyed red lock-head, gripping the dream
That holds good, goes lost in the heaved calm

Of the earth you have entered.

Hawk Roosting

I sit in the top of the wood, my eyes closed.
Inaction, no falsifying dream
Between my hooked head and hooked feet:
Or in sleep rehearse perfect kills and eat.

The convenience of the high trees!
The air's buoyancy and the sun's ray
Are of advantage to me;
And the earth's face upward for my inspection.

My feet are locked upon the rough bark.
It took the whole of Creation
To produce my foot, my each feather:
Now I hold Creation in my foot

Or fly up, and revolve it all slowly –
I kill where I please because it is all mine.
There is no sophistry in my body:
My manners are tearing off heads –

The allotment of death.
For the one path of my flight is direct
Through the bones of the living.
No arguments assert my right:

The sun is behind me.
Nothing has changed since I began.
My eye has permitted no change.
I am going to keep things like this.

The Bull Moses

A hoist up and I could lean over
The upper edge of the high half-door,
My left foot ledged on the hinge, and look in at the byre's
Blaze of darkness: a sudden shut-eyed look
Backward into the head.
                              Blackness is depth
Beyond star. But the warm weight of his breathing,
The ammoniac reek of his litter, the hotly-tongued
Mash of his cud, steamed against me.
Then, slowly, as onto the mind's eye –
The brow like masonry, the deep-keeled neck:
Something come up there onto the brink of the gulf,
Hadn't heard of the world, too deep in itself to be called to,
Stood in sleep. He would swing his muzzle at a fly
But the square of sky where I hung, shouting, waving,
Was nothing to him; nothing of our light
Found any reflection in him.
                              Each dusk the farmer led him
Down to the pond to drink and smell the air,
And he took no pace but the farmer
Led him to take it, as if he knew nothing
Of the ages and continents of his fathers,
Shut, while he wombed, to a dark shed
And steps between his door and the duckpond;
The weight of the sun and the moon and the world
    hammered
To a ring of brass through his nostrils. He would raise
His streaming muzzle and look out over the meadows,
But the grasses whispered nothing awake, the fetch
Of the distance drew nothing to momentum
In the locked black of his powers. He came strolling gently
    back,
Paused neither toward the pig-pens on his right,

Nor toward the cow-byres on his left: something
Deliberate in his leisure, some beheld future
Founding in his quiet.
                    I kept the door wide,
Closed it after him and pushed the bolt.

∠134,835 Ant 821.
                /414

LEABHARLANN CHONTAE Longfoirt

View of a Pig

The pig lay on a barrow dead.
It weighed, they said, as much as three men.
Its eyes closed, pink white eyelashes.
Its trotters stuck straight out.

Such weight and thick pink bulk
Set in death seemed not just dead.
It was less than lifeless, further off.
It was like a sack of wheat.

I thumped it without feeling remorse.
One feels guilty insulting the dead,
Walking on graves. But this pig
Did not seem able to accuse.

It was too dead. Just so much
A poundage of lard and pork.
Its last dignity had entirely gone.
It was not a figure of fun.

Too dead now to pity.
To remember its life, din, stronghold
Of earthly pleasure as it had been,
Seemed a false effort, and off the point.

Too deadly factual. Its weight
Oppressed me – how could it be moved?
And the trouble of cutting it up!
The gash in its throat was shocking, but not pathetic.

Once I ran at a fair in the noise
To catch a greased piglet
That was faster and nimbler than a cat,
Its squeal was the rending of metal.

Pigs must have hot blood, they feel like ovens.
Their bite is worse than a horse's —
They chop a half-moon clean out.
They eat cinders, dead cats.

Distinctions and admirations such
As this one was long finished with.
I stared at it a long time. They were going to scald it,
Scald it and scour it like a doorstep.

November

The month of the drowned dog. After long rain the land
Was sodden as the bed of an ancient lake,
Treed with iron and birdless. In the sunk lane
The ditch – a seep silent all summer –

Made brown foam with a big voice: that, and my boots
On the lane's scrubbed stones, in the gulleyed leaves,
Against the hill's hanging silence;
Mist silvering the droplets on the bare thorns

Slower than the change of daylight.
In a let of the ditch a tramp was bundled asleep;
Face tucked down into beard, drawn in
Under his hair like a hedgehog's. I took him for dead,

But his stillness separated from the death
Of the rotting grass and the ground. A wind chilled,
And a fresh comfort tightened through him,
Each hand stuffed deeper into the other sleeve.

His ankles, bound with sacking and hairy band,
Rubbed each other, resettling. The wind hardened;
A puff shook a glittering from the thorns,
And again the rains' dragging grey columns

Smudged the farms. In a moment
The fields were jumping and smoking; the thorns
Quivered, riddled with the glassy verticals.
I stayed on under the welding cold

Watching the tramp's face glisten and the drops on his coat
Flash and darken. I thought what strong trust
Slept in him – as the trickling furrows slept,
And the thorn-roots in their grip on darkness;

And the buried stones, taking the weight of winter;
The hill where the hare crouched with clenched teeth.
Rain plastered the land till it was shining
Like hammered lead, and I ran, and in the rushing wood

Shuttered by a black oak leaned.
The keeper's gibbet had owls and hawks
By the neck, weasels, a gang of cats, crows:
Some, stiff, weightless, twirled like dry bark bits

In the drilling rain. Some still had their shape,
Had their pride with it; hung, chins on chests,
Patient to outwait these worst days that beat
Their crowns bare and dripped from their feet.

Snowdrop

Now is the globe shrunk tight
Round the mouse's dulled wintering heart.
Weasel and crow, as if moulded in brass,
Move through an outer darkness
Not in their right minds,
With the other deaths. She, too, pursues her ends,
Brutal as the stars of this month,
Her pale head heavy as metal.

Pike

Pike, three inches long, perfect
Pike in all parts, green tigering the gold.
Killers from the egg: the malevolent aged grin.
They dance on the surface among the flies.

Or move, stunned by their own grandeur
Over a bed of emerald, silhouette
Of submarine delicacy and horror.
A hundred feet long in their world.

In ponds, under the heat-struck lily pads –
Gloom of their stillness:
Logged on last year's black leaves, watching upwards.
Or hung in an amber cavern of weeds

The jaws' hooked clamp and fangs
Not to be changed at this date;
A life subdued to its instrument;
The gills kneading quietly, and the pectorals.

Three we kept behind glass,
Jungled in weed: three inches, four,
And four and a half: fed fry to them –
Suddenly there were two. Finally one.

With a sag belly and the grin it was born with.
And indeed they spare nobody.
Two, six pounds each, over two feet long,
High and dry and dead in the willow-herb –

One jammed past its gills down the other's gullet:
The outside eye stared: as a vice locks –
The same iron in this eye
Though its film shrank in death.

A pond I fished, fifty yards across,
Whose lilies and muscular tench
Had outlasted every visible stone
Of the monastery that planted them –

Stilled legendary depth:
It was as deep as England. It held
Pike too immense to stir, so immense and old
That past nightfall I dared not cast

But silently cast and fished
With the hair frozen on my head
For what might move, for what eye might move.
The still splashes on the dark pond,

Owls hushing the floating woods
Frail on my ear against the dream
Darkness beneath night's darkness had freed,
That rose slowly towards me, watching.

Thistles

Against the rubber tongues of cows and the hoeing hands of
   men
Thistles spike the summer air
Or crackle open under a blue-black pressure.

Every one a revengeful burst
Of resurrection, a grasped fistful
Of splintered weapons and Icelandic frost thrust up

From the underground stain of a decayed Viking.
They are like pale hair and the gutturals of dialects.
Every one manages a plume of blood.

Then they grow grey, like men.
Mown down, it is a feud. Their sons appear,
Stiff with weapons, fighting back over the same ground.

Her Husband

Comes home dull with coal-dust deliberately
To grime the sink and foul towels and let her
Learn with scrubbing brush and scrubbing board
The stubborn character of money.

And let her learn through what kind of dust
He has earned his thirst and the right to quench it
And what sweat he has exchanged for his money
And the blood-weight of money. He'll humble her

With new light on her obligations.
The fried, woody chips, kept warm two hours in the oven,
Are only part of her answer.
Hearing the rest, he slams them to the fire back

And is away round the house-end singing
'Come back to Sorrento' in a voice
Of resounding corrugated iron.
Her back has bunched into a hump as an insult.

For they will have their rights.
Their jurors are to be assembled
From the little crumbs of soot. Their brief
Goes straight up to heaven and nothing more is heard of it.

Public Bar TV

On a flaked ridge of the desert

Outriders have found foul water. They say nothing;
With the cactus and the petrified tree
Crouch numbed by a wind howling all
Visible horizons equally empty.

The wind brings dust and nothing
Of the wives, the children, the grandmothers
With the ancestral bones, who months ago
Left the last river,

Coming at the pace of oxen.

Second Glance at a Jaguar

Skinful of bowls he bowls them,
The hip going in and out of joint, dropping the spine
With the urgency of his hurry
Like a cat going along under thrown stones, under cover,
Glancing sideways, running
Under his spine. A terrible, stump-legged waddle
Like a thick Aztec disemboweller,
Club-swinging, trying to grind some square
Socket between his hind legs round,
Carrying his head like a brazier of spilling embers,
And the black bit of his mouth, he takes it
Between his back teeth, he has to wear his skin out,
He swipes a lap at the water-trough as he turns,
Swivelling the ball of his heel on the polished spot,
Showing his belly like a butterfly.
At every stride he has to turn a corner
In himself and correct it. His head
Is like the worn down stump of another whole jaguar,
His body is just the engine shoving it forward,
Lifting the air up and shoving on under,
The weight of his fangs hanging the mouth open,
Bottom jaw combing the ground. A gorged look,
Gangster, club-tail lumped along behind gracelessly,
He's wearing himself to heavy ovals,
Muttering some mantra, some drum-song of murder
To keep his rage brightening, making his skin
Intolerable, spurred by the rosettes, the Cain-brands,
Wearing the spots off from the inside,
Rounding some revenge. Going like a prayer-wheel,
The head dragging forward, the body keeping up,
The hind legs lagging. He coils, he flourishes
The blackjack tail as if looking for a target,
Hurrying through the underworld, soundless.

Fern

Here is the fern's frond, unfurling a gesture,
Like a conductor whose music will now be pause
And the one note of silence
To which the whole earth dances gravely.

The mouse's ear unfurls its trust,
The spider takes up her bequest,
And the retina
Reins the creation with a bridle of water.

And, among them, the fern
Dances gravely, like the plume
Of a warrior returning, under the low hills,

Into his own kingdom.

Theology

No, the serpent did not
Seduce Eve to the apple.
All that's simply
Corruption of the facts.

Adam ate the apple.
Eve ate Adam.
The serpent ate Eve.
This is the dark intestine.

The serpent, meanwhile,
Sleeps his meal off in Paradise –
Smiling to hear
God's querulous calling.

Heptonstall

Black village of gravestones.
Skull of an idiot
Whose dreams die back
Where they were born.

Skull of a sheep
Whose meat melts
Under its own rafters.
Only the flies leave it.

Skull of a bird,
The great geographies
Drained to sutures
Of cracked windowsills.

Life tries.

Death tries.

The stone tries.

Only the rain never tires.

Full Moon and Little Frieda

A cool small evening shrunk to a dog bark and the clank of a
    bucket –
And you listening.
A spider's web, tense for the dew's touch.
A pail lifted, still and brimming – mirror
To tempt a first star to a tremor.

Cows are going home in the lane there, looping the hedges
    with their warm wreaths of breath –
A dark river of blood, many boulders,
Balancing unspilled milk.

'Moon!' you cry suddenly, 'Moon! Moon!'

The moon has stepped back like an artist gazing amazed at a
    work

That points at him amazed

Wodwo

What am I? Nosing here, turning leaves over
Following a faint stain on the air to the river's edge
I enter water. What am I to split
The glassy grain of water looking upward I see the bed
Of the river above me upside down very clear
What am I doing here in mid-air? Why do I find
this frog so interesting as I inspect its most secret
interior and make it my own? Do these weeds
know me and name me to each other have they
seen me before, do I fit in their world? I seem
separate from the ground and not rooted but dropped
out of nothing casually I've no threads
fastening me to anything I can go anywhere
I seem to have been given the freedom
of this place what am I then? And picking
bits of bark off this rotten stump gives me
no pleasure and it's no use so why do I do it
me and doing that have coincided very queerly
But what shall I be called am I the first
have I an owner what shape am I what
shape am I am I huge if I go
to the end on this way past these trees and past these trees
till I get tired that's touching one wall of me
for the moment if I sit still how everything
stops to watch me I suppose I am the exact centre
but there's all this what is it roots
roots roots roots and here's the water
again very queer but I'll go on looking

Two Legends

I

Black was the without eye
Black the within tongue
Black was the heart
Black the liver, black the lungs
Unable to suck in light
Black the blood in its loud tunnel
Black the bowels packed in furnace
Black too the muscles
Striving to pull out into the light
Black the nerves, black the brain
With its tombed visions
Black also the soul, the huge stammer
Of the cry that, swelling, could not
Pronounce its sun.

II

Black is the wet otter's head, lifted.
Black is the rock, plunging in foam.
Black is the gall lying on the bed of the blood.

Black is the earth-globe, one inch under,
An egg of blackness
Where sun and moon alternate their weathers

To hatch a crow, a black rainbow
Bent in emptiness
                              over emptiness
But flying

Examination at the Womb-Door

Who owns these scrawny little feet? *Death.*
Who owns this bristly scorched-looking face? *Death.*
Who owns these still-working lungs? *Death.*
Who owns this utility coat of muscles? *Death.*
Who owns these unspeakable guts? *Death.*
Who owns these questionable brains? *Death.*
All this messy blood? *Death.*
These minimum-efficiency eyes? *Death.*
This wicked little tongue? *Death.*
This occasional wakefulness? *Death.*

Given, stolen, or held pending trial?
Held.

Who owns the whole rainy, stony earth? *Death.*
Who owns all of space? *Death.*

Who is stronger than hope? *Death.*
Who is stronger than the will? *Death.*
Stronger than love? *Death.*
Stronger than life? *Death.*

But who is stronger than death?
                                        Me, evidently.
Pass, Crow.

Crow's First Lesson

God tried to teach Crow how to talk.
'Love,' said God. 'Say, Love.'
Crow gaped, and the white shark crashed into the sea
And went rolling downwards, discovering its own depth.

'No, no,' said God. 'Say Love. Now try it. LOVE.'
Crow gaped, and a bluefly, a tsetse, a mosquito
Zoomed out and down
To their sundry flesh-pots.

'A final try,' said God. 'Now, LOVE.'
Crow convulsed, gaped, retched and
Man's bodiless prodigious head
Bulbed out onto the earth, with swivelling eyes,
Jabbering protest –

And Crow retched again, before God could stop him.
And woman's vulva dropped over man's neck and tightened.
The two struggled together on the grass.
God struggled to part them, cursed, wept –

Crow flew guiltily off.

That Moment

When the pistol muzzle oozing blue vapour
Was lifted away
Like a cigarette lifted from an ashtray

And the only face left in the world
Lay broken
Between hands that relaxed, being too late

And the trees closed forever
And the streets closed forever

And the body lay on the gravel
Of the abandoned world
Among abandoned utilities
Exposed to infinity forever

Crow had to start searching for something to eat.

Crow and the Birds

When the eagle soared clear through a dawn distilling of
   emerald.
When the curlew trawled in seadusk through a chime of
   wineglasses
When the swallow swooped through a woman's song in a
   cavern
And the swift flicked through the breath of a violet

When the owl sailed clear of tomorrow's conscience
And the sparrow preened himself of yesterday's promise
And the heron laboured clear of the Bessemer upglare
And the bluetit zipped clear of lace panties
And the woodpecker drummed clear of the rotovator and the
   rose-farm
And the peewit tumbled clear of the laundromat

While the bullfinch plumped in the apple bud
And the goldfinch bulbed in the sun
And the wryneck crooked in the moon
And the dipper peered from the dewball
Crow spraddled head-down in the beach-garbage, guzzling a
   dropped ice-cream.

In Laughter

Cars collide and erupt luggage and babies
In laughter
The steamer upends and goes under saluting like a stuntman
In laughter
The nosediving aircraft concludes with a boom
In laughter
People's arms and legs fly off and fly on again
In laughter
The haggard mask on the bed rediscovers its pang
In laughter, in laughter
The meteorite crashes
With extraordinarily ill-luck on the pram

The ears and eyes are bundled up
Are folded up in the hair,
Wrapped in the carpet, the wallpaper, tied with the lampflex
Only the teeth work on
And the heart, dancing on in its open cave
Helpless on the strings of laughter

While the tears are nickel-plated and come through doors
    with a bang

And the wails stun with fear
And the bones
Jump from the torment flesh has to stay for

Stagger some distance and fall in full view

Still laughter scampers around on centipede boots
Still it runs all over on caterpillar tread
And rolls back onto the mattress, legs in the air

But it's only human

And finally it's had enough – enough!
And slowly sits up, exhausted,
And slowly starts to fasten buttons,
With long pauses,

Like somebody the police have come for.

Crow's Last Stand

Burning
        burning
                burning
                        there was finally something
The sun could not burn, that it had rendered
Everything down to – a final obstacle
Against which it raged and charred

And rages and chars

Fragment of an Ancient Tablet

Above – the well-known lips, delicately downed.
Below – beard between thighs.

Above – her brow, the notable casket of gems.
Below – the belly with its blood-knot.

Above – many a painful frown.
Below – the ticking bomb of the future.

Above – her perfect teeth, with the hint of a fang at the
    corner.
Below – the millstones of two worlds.

Above – a word and a sigh.
Below – gouts of blood and babies.

Above – the face, shaped like a perfect heart.
Below – the heart's torn face.

Lovesong

He loved her and she loved him
His kisses sucked out her whole past and future or tried to
He had no other appetite
She bit him she gnawed him she sucked
She wanted him complete inside her
Safe and sure forever and ever
Their little cries fluttered into the curtains

Her eyes wanted nothing to get away
Her looks nailed down his hands his wrists his elbows
He gripped her hard so that life
Should not drag her from that moment
He wanted all future to cease
He wanted to topple with his arms round her
Off that moment's brink and into nothing
Or everlasting or whatever there was
Her embrace was an immense press
To print him into her bones
His smiles were the garrets of a fairy palace
Where the real world would never come
Her smiles were spider bites
So he would lie still till she felt hungry
His words were occupying armies
Her laughs were an assassin's attempts
His looks were bullets daggers of revenge
Her glances were ghosts in the corner with horrible secrets
His whispers were whips and jackboots
Her kisses were lawyers steadily writing
His caresses were the last hooks of a castaway
Her love-tricks were the grinding of locks
And their deep cries crawled over the floors
Like an animal dragging a great trap

His promises were the surgeon's gag
Her promises took the top off his skull
She would get a brooch made of it
His vows pulled out all her sinews
He showed her how to make a love-knot
Her vows put his eyes in formalin
At the back of her secret drawer
Their screams stuck in the wall
Their heads fell apart into sleep like the two halves
Of a lopped melon, but love is hard to stop

In their entwined sleep they exchanged arms and legs
In their dreams their brains took each other hostage

In the morning they wore each other's face

The Lovepet

Was it an animal was it a bird?
She stroked it. He spoke to it softly.
She made her voice its happy forest.
He brought it out with sugarlump smiles.
Soon it was licking their kisses.

She gave it the strings of her voice which it swallowed
He gave it the blood of his face it grew eager
She gave it the liquorice of her mouth it began to thrive
He opened the aniseed of his future
And it bit and gulped, grew vicious, snatched
The focus of his eyes
She gave it the steadiness of her hand
He gave it the strength of his spine it ate everything

It began to cry what could they give it
They gave it their calendars it bolted their diaries
They gave it their sleep it gobbled their dreams
Even while they slept
It ate their bodyskin and the muscle beneath
They gave it vows its teeth clashed its starvation
Through every word they uttered

It found snakes under the floor it ate them
It found a spider horror
In their palms and ate it

They gave it double smiles and blank silence
It chewed holes in their carpets
They gave it logic
It ate the colour of their hair
They gave it every argument that would come
They gave it shouting and yelling they meant it
It ate the faces of their children
They gave it their photograph albums they gave it their
   records

It ate the colour of the sun
They gave it a thousand letters they gave it money
It ate their future complete it waited for them
Staring and starving
They gave it screams it had gone too far
It ate into their brains
It ate the roof
It ate lonely stone it ate wind crying famine
It went furiously off

They wept they called it back it could have everything
It stripped out their nerves chewed chewed flavourless
It bit at their numb bodies they did not resist
It bit into their blank brains they hardly knew

It moved bellowing
Through a ruin of starlight and crockery

It drew slowly off they could not move

It went far away they could not speak

Littleblood

O littleblood, hiding from the mountains in the mountains
Wounded by stars and leaking shadow
Eating the medical earth.

O littleblood, little boneless little skinless
Ploughing with a linnet's carcase
Reaping the wind and threshing the stones.

O littleblood, drumming in a cow's skull
Dancing with a gnat's feet
With an elephant's nose with a crocodile's tail.

Grown so wise grown so terrible
Sucking death's mouldy tits.

Sit on my finger, sing in my ear, O littleblood.

The Scream

There was the sun on the wall – my childhood's
Nursery picture. And there my gravestone
Shared my dreams, and ate and drank with me happily.

All day the hawk perfected its craftsmanship
And even through the night the miracle persisted.

Mountains lazed in their smoky camp.
Worms in the ground were doing a good job.

Flesh of bronze, stirred with a bronze thirst,
Like a newborn baby at the breast,
Slept in the sun's mercy.

And the inane weights of iron
That come suddenly crashing into people, out of nowhere,
Only made me feel brave and creaturely.

When I saw little rabbits with their heads crushed on roads
I knew I rode the wheel of the galaxy.

Calves' heads all dew-bristled with blood on counters
Grinned like masks where sun and moon danced.

And my mate with his face sewn up
Where they'd opened it to take something out
Lifted a hand –

He smiled, in half-coma,
A stone temple smile.

Then I, too, opened my mouth to praise –
But a silence wedged my gullet.

Like an obsidian dagger, dry, jag-edged,
A silent lump of volcanic glass,

The scream
Vomited itself.

Bride and Groom Lie Hidden for Three Days

She gives him his eyes, she found them
Among some rubble, among some beetles

He gives her her skin
He just seemed to pull it down out of the air and lay it over
    her
She weeps with fearfulness and astonishment

She has found his hands for him, and fitted them freshly at
    the wrists
They are amazed at themselves, they go feeling all over her

He has assembled her spine, he cleaned each piece carefully
And sets them in perfect order
A superhuman puzzle but he is inspired
She leans back twisting this way and that, using it and
    laughing, incredulous

Now she has brought his feet, she is connecting them
So that his whole body lights up

And he has fashioned her new hips
With all fittings complete and with newly wound coils, all
    shiningly oiled
He is polishing every part, he himself can hardly believe it
They keep taking each other to the sun, they find they can
    easily
To test each new thing at each new step

And now she smooths over him the plates of his skull
So that the joints are invisible
And now he connects her throat, her breasts and the pit of
    her stomach
With a single wire

She gives him his teeth, tying their roots to the centrepin of
   his body

He sets the little circlets on her fingertips

She stitches his body here and there with steely purple silk

He oils the delicate cogs of her mouth

She inlays with deep-cut scrolls the nape of his neck

He sinks into place the inside of her thighs

So, gasping with joy, with cries of wonderment
Like two gods of mud
Sprawling in the dirt, but with infinite care

They bring each other to perfection.

A March Calf

Right from the start he is dressed in his best – his blacks and
   his whites
Little Fauntleroy – quiffed and glossy,
A Sunday suit, a wedding natty get-up,
Standing in dunged straw

Under cobwebby beams, near the mud wall,
Half of him legs,
Shining-eyed, requiring nothing more
But that mother's milk come back often.

Everything else is in order, just as it is.
Let the summer skies hold off, for the moment.
This is just as he wants it.
A little at a time, of each new thing, is best.

Too much and too sudden is too frightening –
When I block the light, a bulk from space,
To let him in to his mother for a suck,
He bolts a yard or two, then freezes,

Staring from every hair in all directions,
Ready for the worst, shut up in his hopeful religion,
A little syllogism
With a wet blue-reddish muzzle, for God's thumb.

You see all his hopes bustling
As he reaches between the worn rails towards
The topheavy oven of his mother.
He trembles to grow, stretching his curl-tip tongue –

What did cattle ever find here
To make this dear little fellow
So eager to prepare himself?
He is already in the race, and quivering to win –

His new purpled eyeball swivel-jerks
In the elbowing push of his plans.
Hungry people are getting hungrier,
Butchers developing expertise and markets,

But he just wobbles his tail – and glistens
Within his dapper profile
Unaware of how his whole lineage
Has been tied up.

He shivers for feel of the world licking his side.
He is like an ember – one glow
Of lighting himself up
With the fuel of himself, breathing and brightening.

Soon he'll plunge out, to scatter his seething joy,
To be present at the grass,
To be free on the surface of such a wideness,
To find himself himself. To stand. To moo.

The River in March

Now the river is rich, but her voice is low.
It is her Mighty Majesty the sea
Travelling among the villages incognito.

Now the river is poor. No song, just a thin mad whisper.
The winter floods have ruined her.
She squats between draggled banks, fingering her rags and
   rubbish.

And now the river is rich. A deep choir.
It is the lofty clouds, that work in heaven,
Going on their holiday to the sea.

The river is poor again. All her bones are showing.
Through a dry wig of bleached flotsam she peers up ashamed
From her slum of sticks.

Now the river is rich, collecting shawls and minerals.
Rain brought fatness, but she takes ninety-nine percent
Leaving the fields just one percent to survive on.

And now she is poor. Now she is East wind sick.
She huddles in holes and corners. The brassy sun gives her a
   headache.
She has lost all her fish. And she shivers.

But now once more she is rich. She is viewing her lands.
A hoard of king-cups spills from her folds, it blazes, it cannot
   be hidden.
A salmon, a sow of solid silver,

Bulges to glimpse it.

Apple Dumps

After the fiesta, the beauty-contests, the drunken wrestling
Of the blossom
Come some small ugly swellings, the dwarfish truths
Of the prizes.

After blushing and confetti, the breeze-blown bridesmaids,
    the shadowed snapshots
Of the trees in bloom
Come the gruelling knuckles, and the cracked housemaid's
    hands,
The workworn morning plainness of apples.

Unearthly was the hope, the wet star melting the gland,
Staggering the offer –
But pawky the real returns, not easy to see,
Dull and leaf-green, hidden, still-bitter, and hard.

The orchard flared wings, a new heaven, a dawn-lipped
    apocalypse
Kissing the sleeper –
The apples emerge, in the sun's black shade, among stricken
    trees,
A straggle of survivors, nearly all ailing.

Barley

Barley grain is like seeds of gold bullion.
When you turn a heap with a shovel it pours
With the heavy magic of wealth.
Every grain is a sleeping princess –
Her kingdom is still to come.
She sleeps with sealed lips.
Each grain is like a mouth sealed
Or an eye sealed.
In each mouth the whole bible of barley.
In each eye, the whole sun of barley.
From each single grain, given time,
You could feed the earth.

You treat them rough, dump them into the drill,
Churn them up with a winter supply
Of fertiliser, and steer out onto the tilth
Trailing your wake of grains.

When the field's finished, fresh-damp,
Its stillness is no longer stillness.
The coverlet has been drawn tight again
But now over breathing and dreams.
And water is already bustling to sponge the newcomers.
And the soil, the ancient nurse,
Is assembling everything they will need.
And the angel of earth
Is flying through the field, kissing each one awake.
But it is a hard nursery.
Night and day all through winter huddling naked
They have to listen to pitiless lessons
Of the freezing constellations
And the rain. If it were not for the sun
Who visits them daily, briefly,
To pray with them, they would lose hope

And give up. With him
They recite the Lord's prayer
And sing a psalm. And sometimes at night
When the moon haunts their field and stares down
Into their beds
They sing a psalm softly together
To keep up their courage.

Once their first leaf shivers they sing less
And start working. They cannot miss a day.
They have to get the whole thing right.
Employed by the earth, employed by the sky,
Employed by barley, to be barley.
And now they begin to show their family beauty.
They come charging over the field, under the wind, like
    warriors –
'Terrible as an army with banners',
Barbaric, tireless, Amazon battalions.

And that's how they win their kingdom.
Then they put on gold, for their coronation.
Each one barbed, feathered, a lithe weapon,
Puts on the crown of her kingdom.
Then the whole fieldful of queens
Swirls in a dance
With their invisible partner, the wind,
Like a single dancer.

That is how barley inherits the kingdom of barley.

Football at Slack

Between plunging valleys, on a bareback of hill
Men in bunting colours
Bounced, and their blown ball bounced.

The blown ball jumped, and the merry-coloured men
Spouted like water to head it.
The ball blew away downwind –

The rubbery men bounced after it.
The ball jumped up and out and hung on the wind
Over a gulf of treetops.
Then they all shouted together, and the ball blew back.

Winds from fiery holes in heaven
Piled the hills darkening around them
To awe them. The glare light
Mixed its mad oils and threw glooms.
Then the rain lowered a steel press.

Hair plastered, they all just trod water
To puddle glitter. And their shouts bobbed up
Coming fine and thin, washed and happy

While the humped world sank foundering
And the valleys blued unthinkable
Under depth of Atlantic depression –

But the wingers leapt, they bicycled in air
And the goalie flew horizontal

And once again a golden holocaust
Lifted the cloud's edge, to watch them.

Sunstruck

The freedom of Saturday afternoons
Starched to cricket dazzle, nagged at a theorem –
Shaggy valley parapets
Pending like thunder, narrowing the spin-bowler's angle.

The click, disconnected, might have escaped –
A six! And the ball slammed flat!
And the bat in flinders! The heart soaring!
And everybody jumping up and running –

Fleeing after the ball, stampeding
Through the sudden hole in Saturday – but
Already clapped into hands and the trap-shout
The ball jerked back to the stumper on its elastic.

Everything collapsed that bit deeper
Towards Monday.

Misery of the brassy sycamores!
Misery of the swans and the hard ripple!

Then again Yes Yes a wild YES –
The bat flashed round the neck in a tight coil,
The stretched shout snatching for the North Sea –
But it fell far short, even of Midgley.

And the legs running for dear life, twinkling white
In the cage of wickets
Were cornered again by the ball, pinned to the crease,
Blocked by the green and white pavilion.

Cross-eyed, mid-stump, sun-descending headache!
Brain sewn into the ball's hide
Hammering at four corners of abstraction
And caught and flung back, and caught, and again caught

To be bounced on baked earth, to be clubbed
Toward the wage-mirage sparkle of mills
Toward Lord Savile's heather
Toward the veto of the poisonous Calder

Till the eyes, glad of anything, dropped
From the bails
Into the bottom of a teacup,
To sandwich crusts for the canal cygnets.

The bowler had flogged himself to a dishclout.
And the burned batsmen returned, with changed faces,
'Like men returned from a far journey',
Under the long glare walls of evening

To the cool sheet and the black slot of home.

When Men Got to the Summit

Light words forsook them.
They filled with heavy silence.

Houses came to support them,
But the hard, foursquare scriptures fractured
And the cracks filled with soft rheumatism.

Streets bent to the task
Of holding it all up
Bracing themselves, taking the strain
Till their vertebrae slipped.

The hills went on gently
Shaking their sieve.

Nevertheless, for some giddy moments
A television
Blinked from the wolf's lookout.

Cock-Crows

I stood on a dark summit, among dark summits –
Tidal dawn was splitting heaven from earth,
The oyster
Opening to taste gold.

And I heard the cock-crows kindling in the valley
Under the mist –
They were sleepy,
Bubbling deep in the valley cauldron.

Then one or two tossed clear, like soft rockets
And sank back again dimming.

Then soaring harder, brighter, higher
Tearing the mist,
Bubble-glistenings flung up and bursting to light
Brightening the undercloud,
The fire-crests of the cocks – the sickle shouts,
Challenge against challenge, answer to answer,
Hooking higher,
Clambering up the sky as they melted,
Hanging smouldering from the night's fringes.

Till the whole valley brimmed with cock-crows,
A magical soft mixture boiling over,
Spilling and sparkling into other valleys

Lobbed-up horse-shoes of glow-swollen metal
From sheds in back-gardens, hen-cotes, farms
Sinking back mistily

Till the last spark died, and embers paled

And the sun climbed into its wet sack
For the day's work

While the dark rims hardened
Over the smoke of towns, from holes in earth.

The Long Tunnel Ceiling

Of the main-road canal bridge
Cradled black stalactite reflections.
That was the place for dark loach!

At the far end, the Moderna blanket factory
And the bushy mask of Hathershelf above it
Peered in through the cell-window.

Lorries from Bradford, baled with plump and towering
Wools and cottons met, above my head,
Lorries from Rochdale, and ground past each other
Making that cavern of air and water tremble –

Suddenly a crash!
The long gleam-ponderous watery echo shattered.

And at last it had begun!
That could only have been a brick from the ceiling!
The bridge was starting to collapse!

But the canal swallowed its scare,
The heavy mirror reglassed itself,
And the black arch gazed up at the black arch.

Till a brick
Rose through its eruption – hung massive
Then slammed back with a shock and a shattering.

An ingot!
Holy of holies! A treasure!
A trout
Nearly as long as my arm, solid
Molten pig of many a bronze loach!

There he lay – lazy – a free lord,
Ignoring me. Caressing, dismissing

The eastward easing traffic of drift,
Master of the Pennine Pass!

Found in some thin glitter among mean gritstone,
High under ferns, high up near sour heather,

Brought down on a midnight cloudburst
In a shake-up of heaven and the hills
When the streams burst with zig-zags and explosions

A seed
Of the wild god now flowering for me
Such a tigerish, dark, breathing lily
Between the tyres, under the tortured axles.

Heptonstall Old Church

A great bird landed here.

Its song drew men out of rock,
Living men out of bog and heather.

Its song put a light in the valleys
And harness on the long moors.

Its song brought a crystal from space
And set it in men's heads.

Then the bird died.

Its giant bones
Blackened and became a mystery.

The crystal in men's heads
Blackened and fell to pieces.

The valleys went out.
The moorland broke loose.

Emily Brontë

The wind on Crow Hill was her darling.
His fierce, high tale in her ear was her secret.
But his kiss was fatal.

Through her dark Paradise ran
The stream she loved too well
That bit her breast.

The shaggy sodden king of that kingdom
Followed through the wall
And lay on her love-sick bed.

The curlew trod in her womb.

The stone swelled under her heart.

Her death is a baby-cry on the moor.

Rain

Rain. Floods. Frost. And after frost, rain.
Dull roof-drumming. Wraith-rain pulsing across purple-
    bare woods
Like light across heaved water. Sleet in it.
And the poor fields, miserable tents of their hedges.
Mist-rain off-world. Hills wallowing
In and out of a grey or silvery dissolution. A farm gleaming,
Then all dull in the near drumming. At field-corners
Brown water backing and brimming in grass.
Toads hop across rain-hammered roads. Every mutilated leaf
    there
Looks like a frog or a rained-out mouse. Cattle
Wait under blackened backs. We drive post-holes.
They half fill with water before the post goes in.
Mud-water spurts as the iron bar slam-burns
The oak stake-head dry. Cows
Tamed on the waste mudded like a rugby field
Stand and watch, come very close for company
In the rain that goes on and on, and gets colder.
They sniff the wire, sniff the tractor, watch. The hedges
Are straggles of gap. A few haws. Every half-ton cow
Sinks to the fetlock at every sliding stride.
They are ruining their field and they know it.
They look out sideways from under their brows which are
Their only shelter. The sunk scrubby wood
Is a pulverized wreck, rain riddles its holes
To the drowned roots. A pheasant looking black
In his waterproofs, bends at his job in the stubble.
The mid-afternoon dusk soaks into
The soaked thickets. Nothing protects them.
The fox corpses lie beaten to their bare bones,
Skin beaten off, brains and bowels beaten out.
Nothing but their blueprint bones last in the rain,

Sodden soft. Round their hay racks, calves
Stand in a shine of mud. The gateways
Are deep obstacles of mud. The calves look up, through
  plastered forelocks,
Without moving. Nowhere they can go
Is less uncomfortable. The brimming world
And the pouring sky are the only places
For them to be. Fieldfares squeal over, sodden
Toward the sodden wood. A raven,
Cursing monotonously, goes over fast
And vanishes in rain-mist. Magpies
Shake themselves hopelessly, hop in the spatter. Misery.
Surviving green of ferns and brambles is tumbled
Like an abandoned scrapyard. The calves
Wait deep beneath their spines. Cows roar
Then hang their noses to the mud.
Snipe go over, invisible in the dusk,
With their squelching cries.

4 December 1973

Tractor

The tractor stands frozen – an agony
To think of. All night
Snow packed its open entrails. Now a head-pincering gale,
A spill of molten ice, smoking snow,
Pours into its steel.
At white heat of numbness it stands
In the aimed hosing of ground-level fieriness.

It defies flesh and won't start.
Hands are like wounds already
Inside armour gloves, and feet are unbelievable
As if the toe-nails were all just torn off.
I stare at it in hatred. Beyond it
The copse hisses – capitulates miserably
In the fleeing, failing light. Starlings,
A dirtier sleetier snow, blow smokily, unendingly, over
Towards plantations eastward.
All the time the tractor is sinking
Through the degrees, deepening
Into its hell of ice.

The starter lever
Cracks its action, like a snapping knuckle.
The battery is alive – but like a lamb
Trying to nudge its solid-frozen mother –
While the seat claims my buttock-bones, bites
With the space-cold of earth, which it has joined
In one solid lump.

I squirt commercial sure-fire
Down the black throat – it just coughs.
It ridicules me – a trap of iron stupidity
I've stepped into. I drive the battery
As if I were hammering and hammering

The frozen arrangement to pieces with a hammer
And it jabbers laughing pain-crying mockingly
Into happy life.

And stands
Shuddering itself full of heat, seeming to enlarge slowly
Like a demon demonstrating
A more-than-usually-complete materialization –
Suddenly it jerks from its solidarity
With the concrete, and lurches towards a stanchion
Bursting with superhuman well-being and abandon
Shouting Where Where?

Worse iron is waiting. Power-lift kneels,
Levers awake imprisoned deadweight,
Shackle-pins bedded in cast-iron cow-shit.
The blind and vibrating condemned obedience
Of iron to the cruelty of iron,
Wheels screeched out of their night-locks –

Fingers
Among the tormented
Tonnage and burning of iron

Eyes
Weeping in the wind of chloroform

And the tractor, streaming with sweat,
Raging and trembling and rejoicing.

31 January 1976

Sketching a Thatcher

Bird-bones is on the roof. Seventy-eight
And still a ladder squirrel,
Three or four nitches at a time, up forty rungs,
Then crabbing out across the traverse,
Cock-crows of insulting banter, liberated
Into his old age, like a royal fool
But still tortured with energy. Thatching
Must be the sinless job. Weathered
Like a weathercock, face bright as a ploughshare,
Skinny forearms of steely cable, batting
The reeds flush, crawling, cliff-hanging,
Lizard-silk of his lizard-skinny hands,
Hands never still, twist of body never still –
Bounds in for a cup of tea, 'Caught you all asleep!'
Markets all the gossip – cynical old goblin
Cackling with wicked joy. Bounds out –
Trips and goes full length, bounces back upright,
'Haven't got the weight to get hurt with!' Cheers
Every departure – 'Off for a drink?' and 'Off
To see his fancy woman again!' – leans from the sky,
Sun-burned-out pale eyes, eyes bleached
As old thatch, in the worn tool of his face,
In his haggard pants and his tired-out shirt –
They can't keep up with him. He just can't
Stop working. 'I don't want the money!' He'd
Prefer a few years. 'Have to sell the house to pay me!'
Alertness built into the bird-stare,
The hook of his nose, bill-hook of his face.
Suns have worn him, like an old sun-tool
Of the day-making, an old shoe-tongue
Of the travelling weathers, the hand-palm, ageless,
Of all winds on all roofs. He lams the roof
And the house quakes. Was everybody

Once like him? He's squirmed through
Some tight cranny of natural selection.
The nut-stick yealm-twist's got into his soul,
He didn't break. He's proof
As his crusty roofs. He ladder-dances
His blood light as spirit. His muscles
Must be clean as horn.
And the whole house
Is more pleased with itself, him on it,
Cresting it, and grooming it, and slapping it
Than if an eagle rested there. Sitting
Drinking his tea, he looks like a tatty old eagle,
And his yelping laugh of derision
Is just like a tatty old eagle's.

Ravens

As we came through the gate to look at the few new lambs
On the skyline of lawn smoothness,
A raven bundled itself into air from midfield
And slid away under hard glistenings, low and guilty.
Sheep nibbling, kneeling to nibble the reluctant nibbled
    grass.
Sheep staring, their jaws pausing to think, then chewing
    again,
Then pausing. Over there a new lamb
Just getting up, bumping its mother's nose
As she nibbles the sugar coating off it
While the tattered banners of her triumph swing and drip
    from her rear-end.
She sneezes and a glim of water flashes from her rear-end.
She sneezes again and again, till she's emptied.
She carries on investigating her new present and seeing how
    it works.
Over here is something else. But you are still interested
In that new one, and its new spark of voice,
And its tininess.
Now over here, where the raven was,
Is what interests you next. Born dead,
Twisted like a scarf, a lamb of an hour or two,
Its insides, the various jellies and crimsons and
    transparencies
And threads and tissues pulled out
In straight lines, like tent ropes
From its upward belly opened like a lamb-wool slipper,
The fine anatomy of silvery ribs on display and the cavity,
The head also emptied through the eye-sockets,
The woolly limbs swathed in birth-yolk and impossible
To tell now which in all this field of quietly nibbling sheep
Was its mother. I explain

That it died being born. We should have been here, to help it.
So it died being born. 'And did it cry?' you cry.
I pick up the dangling greasy weight by the hooves soft as
    dogs' pads
That had trodden only womb-water
And its raven-drawn strings dangle and trail,
Its loose head joggles, and 'Did it cry?' you cry again.
Its two-fingered feet splay in their skin between the pressures
Of my fingers and thumb. And there is another,
Just born, all black, splaying its tripod, inching its new points
Towards its mother, and testing the note
It finds in its mouth. But you have eyes now
Only for the tattered bundle of throwaway lamb.
'Did it cry?' you keep asking, in a three-year-old field-wide
Piercing persistence. 'Oh yes' I say 'it cried.'

Though this one was lucky insofar
As it made the attempt into a warm wind
And its first day of death was blue and warm
The magpies gone quiet with domestic happiness
And skylarks not worrying about anything
And the blackthorn budding confidently
And the skyline of hills, after millions of hard years,
Sitting soft.

    15 April 1974

February 17th

A lamb could not get born. Ice wind
Out of a downpour dishclout sunrise. The mother
Lay on the mudded slope. Harried, she got up
And the blackish lump bobbed at her back-end
Under her tail. After some hard galloping,
Some manoeuvring, much flapping of the backward
Lump head of the lamb looking out,
I caught her with a rope. Laid her, head uphill
And examined the lamb. A blood-ball swollen
Tight in its black felt, its mouth gap
Squashed crooked, tongue stuck out, black-purple,
Strangled by its mother. I felt inside,
Past the noose of mother-flesh, into the slippery
Muscled tunnel, fingering for a hoof,
Right back to the port-hole of the pelvis.
But there was no hoof. He had stuck his head out too early
And his feet could not follow. He should have
Felt his way, tip-toe, his toes
Tucked up under his nose
For a safe landing. So I kneeled wrestling
With her groans. No hand could squeeze past
The lamb's neck into her interior
To hook a knee. I roped that baby head
And hauled till she cried out and tried
To get up and I saw it was useless. I went
Two miles for the injection and a razor.
Sliced the lamb's throat-strings, levered with a knife
Between the vertebrae and brought the head off
To stare at its mother, its pipes sitting in the mud
With all earth for a body. Then pushed
The neck-stump right back in, and as I pushed
She pushed. She pushed crying and I pushed gasping.
And the strength

Of the birth push and the push of my thumb
Against that wobbly vertebra were deadlock,
A to-fro futility. Till I forced
A hand past and got a knee. Then like
Pulling myself to the ceiling with one finger
Hooked in a loop, timing my effort
To her birth push groans, I pulled against
The corpse that would not come. Till it came.
And after it the long, sudden, yolk-yellow
Parcel of life
In a smoking slither of oils and soups and syrups –
And the body lay born, beside the hacked-off head.

17 February 1974

The Day He Died

Was the silkiest day of the young year,
The first reconnaissance of the real spring,
The first confidence of the sun.

That was yesterday. Last night, frost.
And as hard as any of all winter.
Mars and Saturn and the Moon dangling in a bunch
On the hard, littered sky.
Today is Valentine's day.

Earth toast-crisp. The snowdrops battered.
Thrushes spluttering. Pigeons gingerly
Rubbing their voices together, in stinging cold.
Crows creaking, and clumsily
Cracking loose.

The bright fields look dazed.
Their expression is changed.
They have been somewhere awful
And come back without him.

The trustful cattle, with frost on their backs,
Waiting for hay, waiting for warmth,
Stand in a new emptiness.

From now on the land
Will have to manage without him.
But it hesitates, in this slow realization of light,
Childlike, too naked, in a frail sun,
With roots cut
And a great blank in its memory.

A Motorbike

We had a motorbike all through the war
In an outhouse – thunder, flight, disruption
Cramped in rust, under washing, abashed, outclassed
By the Brens, the Bombs, the Bazookas elsewhere.

The war ended, the explosions stopped.
The men surrendered their weapons
And hung around limply.
Peace took them all prisoner.
They were herded into their home towns.
A horrible privation began
Of working a life up out of the avenues
And the holiday resorts and the dance-halls.

Then the morning bus was as bad as any labour truck,
The foreman, the boss, as bad as the S.S.
And the ends of the street and the bends of the road
And the shallowness of the shops and the shallowness of the
  beer
And the sameness of the next town
Were as bad as electrified barbed wire
The shrunk-back war ached in their testicles
And England dwindled to the size of a dog-track.

So there came this quiet young man
And he bought our motorbike for twelve pounds.
And he got it going, with difficulty.
He kicked it into life – it erupted
Out of the six-year sleep, and he was delighted.

A week later, astride it, before dawn,
A misty frosty morning,
He escaped

Into a telegraph pole
On the long straight west of Swinton.

Do not Pick up the Telephone

That plastic Buddha jars out a Karate screech

Before the soft words with their spores
The cosmetic breath of the gravestone

Death invented the phone it looks like the altar of death
Do not worship the telephone
It drags its worshippers into actual graves
With a variety of devices, through a variety of disguised
   voices

Sit godless when you hear the religious wail of the telephone

Do not think your house is a hide-out it is a telephone
Do not think you walk your own road, you walk down a
   telephone
Do not think you sleep in the hand of God you sleep in the
   mouthpiece of a telephone
Do not think your future is yours it waits upon a telephone
Do not think your thoughts are your own thoughts they are
   the toys of the telephone
Do not think these days are days they are the sacrificial
   priests of the telephone
The secret police of the telephone

O phone get out of my house
You are a bad god
Go and whisper on some other pillow
Do not lift your snake head in my house
Do not bite any more beautiful people

You plastic crab
Why is your oracle always the same in the end?
What rake-off for you from the cemeteries?

Your silences are as bad
When you are needed, dumb with the malice of the
    clairvoyant insane
The stars whisper together in your breathing
World's emptiness oceans in your mouthpiece
Stupidly your string dangles into the abysses
Plastic you are then stone a broken box of letters
And you cannot utter
Lies or truth, only the evil one
Makes you tremble with sudden appetite to see somebody
    undone

Blackening electrical connections
To where death bleaches its crystals
You swell and you writhe
You open your Buddha gape
You screech at the root of the house

Do not pick up the detonator of the telephone
A flame from the last day will come lashing out of the
    telephone
A dead body will fall out of the telephone

Do not pick up the telephone

In the Likeness of a Grasshopper

A trap
Waits on the field path.

A wicker contraption, with working parts,
Its spring tensed and set.

So flimsily made, out of grass
(Out of the stems, the joints, the raspy-dry flags).

Baited with a fur-soft caterpillar,
A belly of amorous life, pulsing signals.

Along comes a love-sick, perfume-footed
Music of the wild earth.

The trap, touched by a breath,
Jars into action, its parts blur –

And music cries out.

A sinewy violin
Has caught its violinist.

Cloud-fingered summer, the beautiful trapper,
Picks up the singing cage

And takes out the Song, adds it to the Songs
With which she robes herself, which are her wealth,

Sets her trap again, a yard further on.

New Foal

Yesterday he was nowhere to be found
In the skies or under the skies.

Suddenly he's here – a warm heap
Of ashes and embers, fondled by small draughts.

A star dived from outer space – flared
And burned out in the straw.
Now something is stirring in the smoulder.
We call it a foal.

Still stunned
He has no idea where he is.
His eyes, dew-dusky, explore gloom walls and a glare
    doorspace.
Is this the world?
It puzzles him. It is a great numbness.

He pulls himself together, getting used to the weight of
    things
And to that tall horse nudging him, and to this straw.

He rests
From the first blank shock of light, the empty daze
Of the questions –
What has happened? What am I?

His ears keep on asking, gingerly.

But his legs are impatient,
Recovering from so long being nothing
They are restless with ideas, they start to try a few out,
Angling this way and that,
Feeling for leverage, learning fast –

And suddenly he's up

And stretching – a giant hand
Strokes him from nose to heel
Perfecting his outline, as he tightens
The knot of himself.
                                Now he comes teetering
Over the weird earth. His nose
Downy and magnetic, draws him, incredulous,
Towards his mother. And the world is warm
And careful and gentle. Touch by touch
Everything fits him together.

Soon he'll be almost a horse.
He wants only to be Horse,
Pretending each day more and more Horse
Till he's perfect Horse. Then unearthly Horse
Will surge through him, weightless, a spinning of flame
Under sudden gusts,

It will coil his eyeball and his heel
In a single terror – like the awe
Between lightning and thunderclap.

And curve his neck, like a sea-monster emerging
Among foam,

And fling the new moons through his stormy banner,
And the full moons and the dark moons.

Low Water

                This evening
The river is a beautiful idle woman.

The day's August burn-out has distilled
A heady sundowner.
She lies back, bored and tipsy.

She lolls on her deep couch. And a long thigh
Lifts from the flash of her silks.

Adoring trees, kneeling, ogreish eunuchs
Comb out her spread hair, massage her fingers.

She stretches – and an ecstasy tightens
Over her skin, and deep in her gold body

Thrills spasm and dissolve. She drowses.

Her half-dreams lift out of her, light-minded
Love-pact suicides. Copulation and death.

She stirs her love-potion – ooze of balsam
Thickened with fish-mucus and algae.

You stand under leaves, your feet in shallows.
She eyes you steadily from the beginning of the world.

Go Fishing

Join water, wade in underbeing
Let brain mist into moist earth
Ghost loosen away downstream
Gulp river and gravity

Lose words
Cease
Be assumed into glistenings of lymph
As if creation were a wound
As if this flow were all plasm healing

Be supplanted by mud and leaves and pebbles
By sudden rainbow monster-structures
That materialize in suspension gulping
And dematerialize under pressure of the eye

Be cleft by the sliding prow
Displaced by the hull of light and shadow

Dissolved in earth-wave, the soft sun-shock,
Dismembered in sun-melt

Become translucent – one untangling drift
Of water-mesh, and a weight of earth-taste light
Mangled by wing-shadows
Everything circling and flowing and hover-still

Crawl out over roots, new and nameless
Search for face, harden into limbs

Let the world come back, like a white hospital
Busy with urgency words

Try to speak and nearly succeed
Heal into time and other people

An Eel

The strange part is his head. Her head. The strangely ripened
Domes over the brain, swollen nacelles
For some large containment. Lobed glands
Of some large awareness. Eerie the eel's head.
This full, plum-sleeked fruit of evolution.
Beneath it, her snout's a squashed slipper-face,
The mouth grin-long and perfunctory,
Undershot predatory. And the iris, dirty gold
Distilled only enough to be different
From the olive lode of her body,
The grained and woven blacks. And ringed larger
With a vaguer vision, an earlier eye
Behind her eye, paler, blinder,
Inward. Her buffalo hump
Begins the amazement of her progress.
Her mid-shoulder pectoral fin – concession
To fish-life – secretes itself
Flush with her concealing suit: under it
The skin's a pale exposure of deepest eel
As her belly is, a dulled pearl.
Strangest, the thumb-print skin, the rubberized weave
Of her insulation. Her whole body
Damascened with identity. This is she
Suspends the Sargasso
In her inmost hope. Her life is a cell
Sealed from event, her patience
Global and furthered with love
By the bending stars as if she
Were earth's sole initiate. Alone
In her millions, the moon's pilgrim,
The nun of water.

II

Where does the river come from?
And the eel, the night-mind of water –
The river within the river and opposite –
The night-nerve of water?

Not from the earth's remembering mire
Not from the air's whim
Not from the brimming sun. Where from?

From the bottom of the nothing pool
Sargasso of God
Out of the empty spiral of stars

A glimmering person

Night Arrival of Sea-Trout

Honeysuckle hanging her fangs.
Foxglove rearing her open belly.
Dogrose touching the membrane.

Through the dew's mist, the oak's mass
Comes plunging, tossing dark antlers.

Then a shattering
Of the river's hole, where something leaps out –

An upside-down, buried heaven
Snarls, moon-mouthed, and shivers.

Summer dripping stars, biting at the nape.
Lobworms coupling in saliva.
Earth singing under her breath.

And out in the hard corn a horned god
Running and leaping
With a bat in his drum.

October Salmon

He's lying in poor water, a yard or so depth of poor safety,
Maybe only two feet under the no-protection of an
    outleaning small oak,
Half under a tangle of brambles.

After his two thousand miles, he rests,
Breathing in that lap of easy current
In his graveyard pool.

About six pounds weight,
Four years old at most, and hardly a winter at sea –
But already a veteran,
Already a death-patched hero. So quickly it's over!

So briefly he roamed the gallery of marvels!
Such sweet months, so richly embroidered into earth's
    beauty-dress,
Her life-robe –
Now worn out with her tirelessness, her insatiable quest,
Hangs in the flow, a frayed scarf –

An autumnal pod of his flower,
The mere hull of his prime, shrunk at shoulder and flank,

With the sea-going Aurora Borealis
Of his April power –
The primrose and violet of that first upfling in the estuary –
Ripened to muddy dregs,
The river reclaiming his sea-metals.

In the October light
He hangs there, patched with leper-cloths.

Death has already dressed him
In her clownish regimentals, her badges and decorations,
Mapping the completion of his service,

His face a ghoul-mask, a dinosaur of senility, and his whole
    body
A fungoid anemone of canker –

Can the caress of water ease him?
The flow will not let up for a minute.

What a change! from that covenant of polar light
To this shroud in a gutter!
What a death-in-life – to be his own spectre!
His living body become death's puppet,
Dolled by death in her crude paints and drapes
He haunts his own staring vigil
And suffers the subjection, and the dumbness,
And the humiliation of the role!

And that is how it is,
That is what is going on there, under the scrubby oak tree,
    hour after hour,
That is what the splendour of the sea has come down to,
And the eye of ravenous joy – king of infinite liberty
In the flashing expanse, the bloom of sea-life,

On the surge-ride of energy, weightless,
Body simply the armature of energy
In that earliest sea-freedom, the savage amazement of life,
The salt mouthful of actual existence
With strength like light –

Yet this was always with him. This was inscribed in his egg.
This chamber of horrors is also home.
He was probably hatched in this very pool.

And this was the only mother he ever had, this uneasy
    channel of minnows
Under the mill-wall, with bicycle wheels, car tyres, bottles
And sunk sheets of corrugated iron.
People walking their dogs trail their evening shadows across
    him.

If boys see him they will try to kill him.

All this, too, is stitched into the torn richness,
The epic poise
That holds him so steady in his wounds, so loyal to his doom, so patient
In the machinery of heaven.

That Morning

We came where the salmon were so many
So steady, so spaced, so far-aimed
On their inner map, England could add

Only the sooty twilight of South Yorkshire
Hung with the drumming drift of Lancasters
Till the world had seemed capsizing slowly.

Solemn to stand there in the pollen light
Waist-deep in wild salmon swaying massed
As from the hand of God. There the body

Separated, golden and imperishable,
From its doubting thought – a spirit-beacon
Lit by the power of the salmon

That came on, came on, and kept on coming
As if we flew slowly, their formations
Lifting us toward some dazzle of blessing

One wrong thought might darken. As if the fallen
World and salmon were over. As if these
Were the imperishable fish

That had let the world pass away –

There, in a mauve light of drifted lupins,
They hung in the cupped hands of mountains

Made of tingling atoms. It had happened.
Then for a sign that we were where we were
Two gold bears came down and swam like men

Beside us. And dived like children.
And stood in deep water as on a throne
Eating pierced salmon off their talons.

So we found the end of our journey.

So we stood, alive in the river of light
Among the creatures of light, creatures of light.

Little Whale Song
for Charles Causley

What do they think of themselves
With their global brains –
The tide-power voltage illumination
Of those brains? Their X-ray all-dimension

Grasp of this world's structures, their brains budded
Clone replicas of the electron world
Lit and re-imagining the world,
Perfectly tuned receivers and perceivers,

Each one a whole tremulous world
Feeling through the world? What
Do they make of each other?

'We are beautiful. We stir

Our self-colour in the pot of colours
Which is the world. At each
Tail-stroke we deepen
Our being into the world's lit substance,

And our joy into the world's
Spinning bliss, and our peace
Into the world's floating, plumed peace.'

Their body-tons, echo-chambered,

Amplify the whisper
Of currents and airs, of sea-peoples

And planetary manoeuvres,
Of seasons, of shores, and of their own

Moon-lifted incantation, as they dance
Through the original Earth-drama
In which they perform, as from the beginning,

The Royal House.
                          The loftiest, spermiest

Passions, the most exquisite pleasures,
The noblest characters, the most god-like
Oceanic presence and poise –

The most terrible fall.

Rain-Charm for the Duchy
for H.R.H. Prince Harry

After the five-month drought
My windscreen was frosted with dust.
Sight itself had grown a harsh membrane
Against glare and particles.

Now the first blobby tears broke painfully.

Big, sudden thunderdrops. I felt them sploshing like vapoury
   petrol
Among the ants
In Cranmere's cracked heath-tinder. And into the ulcer craters
Of what had been river pools.

Then, like taking a great breath, we were under it.
Thunder gripped and picked up the city.
Rain didn't so much fall as collapse.
The pavements danced, like cinders in a riddle.

Flash in the pan, I thought, as people scampered.
Soon it was falling vertical, precious, pearled.
Thunder was a brass-band accompaniment
To some festive, civic event. Squeals and hurry. With tourist
   bunting.

The precinct saplings lifted their arms and faces. And the
   heaped-up sky
Moved in mayoral pomp, behind buildings,
With flash and thump. It had almost gone by
And I almost expected the brightening. Instead, something
   like a shutter

Jerked and rattled – and the whole county darkened.
Then rain really came down. You scrambled into the car
Scattering oxygen like a drenched bush.
What a weight of warm Atlantic water!

The car-top hammered. The Cathedral jumped in and out
Of a heaven that had obviously caught fire
And couldn't be contained.
A girl in high heels, her handbag above her head,

Risked it across the square's lit metals.
We saw surf cuffed over her and the car jounced.
Grates, gutters, clawed in the backwash.
She kept going. Flak and shrapnel

Of thundercracks
Hit the walls and roofs. Still a swimmer
She bobbed off, into sea-smoke,
Where headlights groped. Already

Thunder was breaking up the moors.
It dragged tors over the city –
Uprooted chunks of map. Smeltings of ore, pink and violet,
Spattered and wriggled down

Into the boiling sea
Where Exeter huddled –
A small trawler, nets out.
'Think of the barley!' you said.

You remembered earlier harvests.
But I was thinking
Of joyful sobbings –
The throb

In the rock-face mosses of the Chains,
And of the exultant larvae in the Barle's shrunk trench, their
    filaments ablur like propellers, under the churned ceiling
    of light,

And of the Lyn's twin gorges, clearing their throats,
    deepening their voices, beginning to hear each other
Rehearse forgotten riffles,

And the Mole, a ditch's choked whisper
Rousing the stagnant camps of the Little Silver, the Crooked
   Oak and the Yeo
To a commotion of shouts, muddied oxen
A rumbling of wagons,

And the red seepage, the smoke of life
Lowering its ringlets into the Taw,

And the Torridge, rising to the kiss,
Plunging under sprays, new-born,
A washed cherub, clasping the breasts of light,

And the Okement, nudging her detergent bottles, tugging at
   her nylon stockings, starting to trundle her Pepsi-Cola
   cans,

And the Tamar, roused and blinking under the fifty-mile
   drumming,
Declaiming her legend – her rusty knights tumbling out of
   their clay vaults, her cantrevs assembling from shillets,
With a cheering of aged stones along the Lyd and the Lew,
   the Wolf and the Thrushel,

And the Tavy, jarred from her quartzy rock-heap, feeling the
   moor shift
Rinsing her stale mouth, tasting tin, copper, ozone,

And the baby Erme, under the cyclone's top-heavy, toppling
   sea-fight, setting afloat odd bits of dead stick,

And the Dart, her shaggy horde coming down
Astride bareback ponies, with a cry,
Loosening sheepskin banners, bumping the granite,
Flattening rowans and frightening oaks,

And the Teign, startled in her den
By the rain-dance of bracken
Hearing Heaven reverberate under Gidleigh,

And the highest pool of the Exe, her coil recoiling under the
   sky-shock
Where a drinking stag flings its head up
From a spilled skyful of lightning –

My windscreen wipers swam as we moved.
                                   I imagined the two moors
The two stone-age hands
Cupped and brimming, lifted, an offering –
And I thought of those other, different lightnings, the
   patient, thirsting ones

Under Crow Island, inside Bideford Bar,
And between the Hamoaze anchor chains,
And beneath the thousand, shivering, fibreglass hulls
Inside One Gun Point, and aligned

Under the Ness, and inside Great Bull Hill:

The salmon, deep in the thunder, lit
And again lit, with glimpses of quenchings,
Twisting their glints in the suspense,
Biting at the stir, beginning to move.

The Last of the 1st/5th Lancashire Fusiliers
A Souvenir of the Gallipoli Landings

The father capers across the yard cobbles
Look, like a bird, a water-bird, an ibis going over pebbles
We laughed, like warships fluttering bunting.

Heavy-duty design, deep-seated in ocean-water
The warships flutter bunting.
A fiesta day for the warships
Where war is only an idea, as drowning is only an idea
In the folding of a wave, in the mourning
Funeral procession, the broadening wake
That follows a ship under power.

War is an idea in the muzzled calibre of the big guns.
In the grey, wolvish outline.
War is a kind of careless health, like the heart-beat
In the easy bodies of sailors, feeling the big engines
Idling between emergencies.

It is what has left the father
Who has become a bird.
Once he held war in his strong pint mugful of tea
And drank at it, heavily sugared.
It was all for him
Under the parapet, under the periscope, the look-out
Under Achi Baba and the fifty billion flies.

Now he has become a long-billed, spider-kneed bird
Bow-backed, finding his footing, over the frosty cobbles
A wader, picking curiosities from the shallows.

His sons don't know why they laughed, watching him
    through the window
Remembering it, remembering their laughter
They only want to weep

As after the huge wars

Senseless huge wars

Huge senseless weeping.

Football

I was sick of football
Before I understood
What the game was. Dad and his boyhood!
Something his feet seemed to ail.

That damned tin can he had to kick
The whole way daily to school
Then the whole way back! His iron-shod rule.
Like a blind man with a white stick.

The school handbell, rung for playtime to end,
Flew off its handle. The purest chance.
His boot couldn't resist it – mid-bounce
He put it straight through a classroom window.

A puppy-dog, in the fish and chip shop,
Jumped from somebody's arms. It was bolting
Out for the street as his foot saved it. Incredible!
It soared over the counter into the chip-fat.

Impossible! But he did it – his boot did it
While he stared appalled. Then endless
Endless running on the hills
Escaping the torment of unfitness.

Centre half, the local team,
Picked by the talent scout for the big time
Just as the trenches buried him. More muscular
He emerged a Catch-as-catch-can wrestler.

Demobbed, he'd lost patience as a footman
Of the field's niceties.
More an assault-force with a grudge for justice,
The hit-man for the opposition's hit-men.

During his last game, my brother
Crept at half-time from the crowd
That was roaring for his father's blood.
His quiet father. His gentle, thunderstorm father.

Using up his family's every last kick.
His game, the Great War – one and synonymous.
His field – our burnt-out-no-man's-land. His trophies –
Our crosses. His triumphs – our after-shock.

Comics

My brother was born blue with his head jammed
Hard against the stony dead-end
Of the industrial tunnel. The birth-cord
Tight around his neck. His escape tool
Was Comics, Westerns. Freedom
Opened away North of the Great Divide
Inside the head. His talisman, his compass,
The rifle
Fallen into his hands from the Paleolithic,
Invisibly engraved
With Bison and Cave Bear. But the Comic Mags
Collected anyhow
Were the drug that took him
Up through the smoke-hole, out through the attic skylight.

Mother feared their visions.
The Wesleyan prudery of her girlhood –
Or what? – again and again she crammed them
Into the ash-bin. Again and again he retrieved them –
Stock to trade for others. She feared
The stars in the eyes, the bear path
Leading out of the valley
Into the den of a strange woman. The snare
Of a temple harlot.
The wrong gods. 'If you do this, that or that –
You'll kill me. Those Magazines
Are my dreams being torn into tiny pieces
By godless men who dream of bad women –
This valley and all its works, all we've slaved for,
Dumped in the ash-bin. Chapels and godliness,
Next to cleanliness, torn up and dumped in an ash-bin.'

That is what she meant, dumping his comics –
As if they were true maps

Locating Gold Fields sown with spent bullets
And upturned toes. Or Paradise East of the Sun.
Or the folly-stone of the Alchemists
In a nest of hocus-pocus.
She didn't know what she was doing
That was so clairvoyant –
As when she clawed in the blazing coals
For a screwed up ten shilling note she'd idly tossed there –
Only knowing that she was desperate
And that it was all too late.

Midas

Peasants crowded to gawp at Silenus –
The end-product of a life
They could not imagine.
They chained him with flowers and dragged him,
In a harness of flowers, to their king, Midas,
As if he were some
Harmless, helpless, half-tapir or other
Charming monster.
When Midas recognised him,
And honoured him, fat and old and drunk as he was,
As the companion of Bacchus,
And restored him to the god,

Bacchus was so grateful
He offered to grant Midas any wish –
Whatever the King wanted, it would be granted.
Midas was overjoyed
To hear this first approach, so promising,
Of his peculiar horrible doom.
He did not have to rack his brains.
A certain fantasy
Hovered in his head perpetually,
Wistfully fondled all his thoughts by day,
Manipulated all his dreams by night.
Now it saw its chance and seized his tongue.
It shoved aside
The billion – infinite – opportunities
For Midas
To secure a happiness, guaranteed,
Within the human range
Of what is possible to a god.
It grasped, with a king's inane greed,
The fate I shall describe.

Midas said: 'Here is my wish.
Let whatever I touch become gold.
Yes, gold, the finest, the purest, the brightest.'
Bacchus gazed at the King and sighed gently.
He felt pity –
Yet his curiosity was intrigued
To see how such stupidity would be punished.
So he granted the wish, then stood back to watch.

The Phrygian King returned through the garden
Eager to test the power – yet apprehensive
That he had merely dreamed and now was awake,
Where alchemy never works. He broke a twig
From a low branch of oak. The leaves
Turned to heavy gold as he stared at them
And his mouth went dry.
He felt his brain move strangely, like a muscle.
He picked up a stone and weighed it in his hand
As it doubled its weight, then doubled it again,
And became bright yellow.
He brushed his hand over a clump of grass,
The blades stayed bent – soft ribbons
Of gold foil. A ripe ear of corn
Was crisp and dry and light as he plucked it
But a heavy slug of gold, intricately braided
As he rolled it between his palms.
It was then that a cold thought seemed to whisper.
He had wanted to chew the milky grains –
But none broke chaffily free from their pockets.
The ear was gold – its grain inedible,
Inaccessibly solid with the core.
He frowned. With the frown on his face
He reached for a hanging apple.
With a slight twist he took the sudden weight
No longer so happily. This was a fruit
He made no attempt to bite, as he pondered its colour.

Almost inadvertently he stroked
The door pillars, as he entered the palace,
Pausing to watch the brilliant yellow
Suffuse the dark stone.
He washed his hands under flowing water, at a fountain.
Already a hope
Told him that the gift might wash away,
As waking up will wash out a nightmare.
But the water that touched him
Coiled into the pool below as plumes
Of golden smoke, settling heavily
In a silt of gold atoms.

Suddenly his vision
Of transmuting his whole kingdom to gold
Made him sweat –
It chilled him as he sat
At the table
And reached for a roasted bird. The carcase
Toppled from his horrified fingers
Into his dish with a clunk,
As if he had picked up a table ornament.
He reached for bread
But could not break
The plaque of gold that resembled a solid puddle
Smelted from ore.
Almost in terror now
He reached for the goblet of wine –
Taking his time, he poured in water,
Swirled the mix in what had been translucent
Rhinoceros horn
But was already common and commoner metal.
He set his lips to the cold rim
And others, dumbfounded
By what they had already seen, were aghast
When they saw the wet gold shine on his lips,

And as he lowered the cup
Saw him mouthing gold, spitting gold mush –
That had solidified, like gold cinders.
He got up, reeling
From his golden chair, as if poisoned.

He fell on his bed, face down, eyes closed
From the golden heavy fold of his pillow.
He prayed
To the god who had given him the gift
To take it back. 'I have been a fool.
Forgive me, Bacchus. Forgive the greed
That made me so stupid.
Forgive me for a dream
That had not touched the world
Where gold is truly gold and nothing but.
Save me from my own shallowness,
Where I shall drown in gold
And be buried in gold.
Nothing can live, I see, in a world of gold.'

Bacchus, too, had had enough.
His kindliness came uppermost easily.
'I return you,' said the god,
'To your happier human limitations.
But now you must wash away
The last stain of the curse
You begged for and preferred to every blessing.
A river goes by Sardis. Follow it upstream.
Find the source
Which gushes from a cliff and plunges
Into a rocky pool. Plunge with it.
Go completely under. Let that river
Carry your folly away and leave you clean.'

Midas obeyed and the river's innocent water
Took whatever was left of the granted wish.

Even today the soil of its flood plain
Can be combed into a sparse glitter.
And big popcorns of gold, in its gravels,
Fever the fossicker.

Midas never got over the shock.
The sight of gold was like the thought of a bee
To one just badly stung –
It made his hair prickle, his nerves tingle.
He retired to the mountain woods
And a life of deliberate poverty. There
He worshipped Pan, who lives in the mountain caves.
King Midas was chastened
But not really changed. He was no wiser.
His stupidity
Was merely lying low. Waiting, as usual,
For another chance to ruin his life.

*

The cliff-face of Tmolus watches
Half the Mediterranean. It falls away
To Sardis on one side, and on the other
To the village of Hypaepa.
Pan lives in a high cave on that cliff.
He was amusing himself,
Showing off to the nymphs
Thrilling them out of their airy bodies
With the wild airs
He breathed through the reeds of his flute.
Their ecstasies flattered him,
Their words, their exclamations, flattered him.
But the flattered
Become fools. And when he assured them
That Apollo, no less,
Stole his tunes and rearranged his rhythms

It was a shock
For Pan
To find himself staring at the great god
Hanging there in the air off the cave mouth,
Half eclipsed with black rage,
Half beaming with a friendly challenge.
'Tmolus, the mountain,' suggested the god, 'can judge us.'

Tmolus shook out his hair,
Freed his ears of bushes, trees, bird, insects,
Then took his place at the seat of judgement,
Binding his wig with a whole oak tree –
The acorns clustering over his eyebrows,
And announced to Pan: 'Your music first.'

It so happened
Midas was within hearing
Collecting nuts and berries. Suddenly he heard
Music that froze him immobile
As long as it lasted. He did not know
What happened to him as Pan's piping
Carried him off –
Filled him with precipices,
Lifted him on weathered summits,
Poured blue icy rivers through him,
Hung him from the stars,
Replaced him
With the fluorescent earth
Spinning and dancing on the jet of a fountain.

It stopped, and Tmolus smiled,
As if coming awake –
Back, he thought, hugely refreshed
From a journey through himself.
But now he turned
To Apollo, the great, bright god.

As he turned, all his forests
Dragged like a robe.

Apollo was serious.
His illustrious hair burst
From under a wreath of laurel picked
Only moments ago on Parnassus.
The fringe of his cloak of Tyrian purple
Was all that touched the earth.
In his left hand the lyre
Was a model, in magical code,
Of the earth and the heavens –
Ivory of narwhal and elephant,
Diamonds from the interiors of stars.
In his right hand he held
The plectrum that could touch
Every wavelength in the Universe
Singly or simultaneously.
Even his posture
Was like a tone – like a tuning fork,
Vibrant, alerting the whole earth,
Bringing heaven down to listen.

Then the plectrum moved and Tmolus,
After the first chords,
Seemed to be about to decompose
Among the harmonics.
He pulled himself together – but it was no use,
He was helpless
As the music dissolved him and poured him
Through the snakes and ladders
Of the creation and the decreation
Of the elements,
And finally, bringing the sea-horizon
To an edge clean as a knife,
Restored him to his shaggy, crumpled self.

Pan was humbled. Yes, he agreed –
Apollo was the master. Tmolus was correct.
The nymphs gazed at Apollo. They agreed.
But then a petulant voice,
A hard-angled, indignant, differing voice
Came from behind a rock.

Midas stood up. 'The judgement,' he cried,
'Is ignorant, stupid, and merely favours power.
Apollo's efforts
Are nothing but interior decoration
By artificial light, for the chic, the effete.
Pan is the real thing – the true voice
Of the subatomic.'

Apollo's face seemed to writhe
Momentarily
As he converted this clown's darkness to light,
Then pointed his plectrum at the ears
That had misheard so grievously.

Abruptly those ears lolled long and animal,
On either side of Midas' impertinent face.
Revolving at the root, grey-whiskered, bristly,
The familiar ears of a big ass.
The King,
Feeling the change, grabbed to hang on to his ears.
Then he had some seconds of pure terror
Waiting for the rest of his body to follow.
But the ears used up the power of the plectrum.
This was the god's decision. The King
Lived on, human, wagging the ears of a donkey.

Midas crept away.
Every few paces he felt at his ears and groaned.
He slunk back to his palace. He needed
Comfort. He was bitterly disillusioned
With the spirit of the wilderness.

He hid those ears – in a turban superb
As compensation could be.

But a king needs a barber.
Sworn to secrecy or impalement
The barber, wetting his lips,
Clipped around the gristly roots
Of the great angling ears as if the hair there
Might be live nerve-ends.
What he was staring at,
And having to believe, was worse
For him than for their owner,
Almost. He had to hide this news
As if it were red-hot
Under his tongue, and keep it there.
The ultimate shame secret
Of the ruler of the land.
It struggled to blurt
Itself out, whenever
He opened his mouth.
It made him sweat and often
Gasp aloud, or strangle
A groan to a sigh. Or wake up
In the middle of the silent night
Certain he had just
Yelled it out, at the top of his voice,
To the whole city.
He knew, this poor barber,
He had to spit it out somehow.

In the lawn of a park he lifted a turf
After midnight. He kneeled there
And whispered into the raw hole
'Ass's ears! Midas has ass's ears!'
Then fitted the turf back, trod flat the grave
Of that insuppressible gossip,

And went off, singing
Under his breath.

But in no time,
As if the barber had grafted it there
From some far-off reed-bed,
A clump of reeds bunched out, from that very sod.
It looked strange, on the park lawn,
But sounded stranger.
Every gust brought an articulate whisper
Out of the bending stalks. At every puff
They betrayed the barber's confidence,
Broadcasting the buried secret.
Hissing to all who happened to be passing:
'Ass's ears! Midas has ass's ears!'

The Tender Place

Your temples, where the hair crowded in,
Were the tender place. Once to check
I dropped a file across the electrodes
Of a twelve-volt battery – it exploded
Like a grenade. Somebody wired you up.
Somebody pushed the lever. They crashed
The thunderbolt into your skull.
In their bleached coats, with blenched faces,
They hovered again
To see how you were, in your straps.
Whether your teeth were still whole.
The hand on the calibrated lever
Again feeling nothing
Except feeling nothing pushed to feel
Some squirm of sensation. Terror
Was the cloud of you
Waiting for these lightnings. I saw
An oak limb sheared at a bang.
You your Daddy's leg. How many seizures
Did you suffer this god to grab you
By the roots of the hair? The reports
Escaped back into clouds. What went up
Vaporized? Where lightning rods wept copper
And the nerve threw off its skin
Like a burning child
Scampering out of the bomb-flash. They dropped you
A rigid bent bit of wire
Across the Boston City grid. The lights
In the Senate House dipped
As your voice dived inwards

Right through the bolt-hole basement.
Came up, years later,

Over-exposed, like an X-ray –
Brain-map still dark-patched
With the scorched-earth scars
Of your retreat. And your words,
Faces reversed from the light,
Holding in their entrails.

Fate Playing

Because the message somehow met a goblin,
Because precedents tripped your expectations,
Because your London was still a kaleidoscope
Of names and places any jolt could scramble,
You waited mistaken. The bus from the North
Came in and emptied and I was not on it.
No matter how much you insisted
And begged the driver, probably with tears,
To produce me or to remember seeing me
Just miss getting on. I was not on it.
Eight in the evening and I was lost and at large
Somewhere in England. You restrained
Your confident inspiration
And did not dash out into the traffic
Milling around Victoria, utterly certain
Of bumping into me where I would have to be walking.
I was not walking anywhere. I was sitting
Unperturbed, in my seat on the train
Rocking towards King's Cross. Somebody,
Calmer than you, had a suggestion. So,
When I got off the train, expecting to find you
Somewhere down at the root of the platform,
I saw that surge and agitation, a figure
Breasting the flow of released passengers,
Then your molten face, your molten eyes
And your exclamations, your flinging arms
Your scattering tears
As if I had come back from the dead
Against every possibility, against
Every negative but your own prayer
To your own gods. There I knew what it was
To be a miracle. And behind you
Your jolly taxi-driver, laughing, like a small god,

To see an American girl being so American,
And to see your frenzied chariot-ride –
Sobbing and goading him, and pleading with him
To make happen what you needed to happen –
Succeed so completely, thanks to him.
Well, it was a wonder
That my train was not earlier, even much earlier,
That it pulled in, late, the very moment
You irrupted onto the platform. It was
Natural and miraculous and an omen
Confirming everything
You wanted confirmed. So your huge despair,
Your cross-London panic dash
And now your triumph, splashed over me,
Like love forty-nine times magnified,
Like the first thunder cloudburst engulfing
The drought in August
When the whole cracked earth seems to quake
And every leaf trembles
And everything holds up its arms weeping.

You Hated Spain

                              Spain frightened you. Spain
Where I felt at home. The blood-raw light,
The oiled anchovy faces, the African
Black edges to everything, frightened you.
Your schooling had somehow neglected Spain.
The wrought-iron grille, death and the Arab drum.
You did not know the language, your soul was empty
Of the signs, and the welding light
Made your blood shrivel. Bosch
Held out a spidery hand and you took it
Timidly, a bobby-sox American.
You saw right down to the Goya funeral grin
And recognized it, and recoiled
As your poems winced into chill, as your panic
Clutched back towards college America.
So we sat as tourists at the bullfight
Watching bewildered bulls awkwardly butchered,
Seeing the grey-faced matador, at the barrier
Just below us, straightening his bent sword
And vomiting with fear. And the horn
That hid itself inside the blowfly belly
Of the toppled picador punctured
What was waiting for you. Spain
Was the land of your dreams: the dust-red cadaver
You dared not wake with, the puckering amputations
No literature course had glamorized.
The juju land behind your African lips.
Spain was what you tried to wake up from
And could not. I see you, in moonlight,
Walking the empty wharf at Alicante
Like a soul waiting for the ferry,
A new soul, still not understanding,
Thinking it is still your honeymoon

In the happy world, with your whole life waiting,
Happy, and all your poems still to be found.

The Earthenware Head

Who modelled your head of terracotta?
Some American student friend.
Life-size, the lips half-pursed, raw-edged
With crusty tooling – a naturalistic attempt
At a likeness that just failed. You did not like it.
I did not like it. Unease magnetized it
For a perverse rite. What possessed us
To take it with us, in your red bucket bag?
November fendamp haze, the river unfurling
Dark whorls, ferrying slender willow yellows.
The pollard willows wore comfortless antlers,
Switch-horns, leafless. Just past where the field
Broadens and the path strays up to the right
To lose the river and puzzle for Grantchester,
A chosen willow leaned towards the water.
Above head height, the socket of a healed bole-wound,
A twiggy crotch, nearly an owl's porch,
Made a mythic shrine for your double.
I fitted it upright, firm. And a willow tree
Was a Herm, with your head, watching East
Through those tool-stabbed pupils. We left it
To live the world's life and weather forever.

You ransacked Thesaurus in your poem about it,
Veiling its mirror, rhyming yourself into safety
From its orphaned fate.
But it would not leave you. Weeks later
We could not seem to hit on the tree. We did not
Look too hard – just in passing. Already
You did not want to fear, if it had gone,
What witchcraft might ponder it. You never
Said much more about it.
                    What happened?

Maybe nothing happened. Perhaps
It is still there, representing you
To the sunrise, and happy
In its cold pastoral, lips pursed slightly
As if my touch had only just left it.
Or did boys find it – and shatter it? Or
Did the tree too kneel finally?
Surely the river got it. Surely
The river is its chapel. And keeps it. Surely
Your deathless head, fired in a furnace,
Face to face at last, kisses the Father
Mudded at the bottom of the Cam,
Beyond recognition or rescue,
All our fears washed from it, and perfect,
Under the stained mournful flow, saluted
Only in summer briefly by the slender
Punt-loads of shadows flitting towards their honey
And the stopped clock.
                              Evil.
That was what you called the head. Evil.

Flounders

Was that a happy day? From Chatham
Down at the South end of the Cape, our map
Somebody's optimistic assurance,
We set out to row. We got ourselves
Into mid-channel. The tide was flowing. We hung
Anchored. Northward-pulling, our baited leads
Bounced and bounced the bottom. For three hours –
Two or three sea-robins. Cruisers
Folded us under their bow-waves, we bobbed up,
Happy enough. But the wind
Smartened against us, and the tide turned, roughening,
Dragged seaward. We rowed. We rowed. We
Saw we weren't going to make it. We turned,
Cutting downwind for the sand-bar, beached
And wondered what next. It was there
I found a horse-shoe crab's carapace, perfect,
No bigger than a bee, in honey-pale cellophane.
No way back. But big, good America found us.
A power-boat and a pilot of no problems.
He roped our boat to his stern and with all his family
Slammed back across the channel into the wind,
The spray scything upwards, our boat behind
Twisting across the wake-boil – a hectic
Four or five minutes and he cast us off
In the lee of the land, but a mile or more
From our dock. We toiled along inshore. We came
To a back-channel, under beach-house gardens – marsh
    grass,
Wild, original greenery of America,
Mud-slicks and fiddler-crab warrens, as we groped
Towards the harbour. Gloom-rich water. Something
Suggested easy plenty. We lowered baits,
And out of about six feet of water

Six or seven feet from land, we pulled up flounders
Big as big plates, till all our bait had gone.
After our wind-burned, head-glitter day of emptiness,
And the slogging row for our lives, and the rescue,
Suddenly out of water easy as oil
The sea piled our boat with its surplus. And the day
Curled out of brilliant, arduous morning,
Through wind-hammered perilous afternoon,
Salt-scoured, to a storm-gold evening, a luxury
Of rowing among the dream-yachts of the rich
Lolling at anchor off the play-world pier.

How tiny an adventure
To stay so monumental in our marriage,
A slight ordeal of all that might be,
And a small thrill-breath of what many live by,
And a small prize, a toy miniature
Of the life that might have bonded us
Into a single animal, a single soul –

It was a visit from the goddess, the beauty
Who was poetry's sister – she had come
To tell poetry she was spoiling us.
Poetry listened, maybe, but we heard nothing
And poetry did not tell us. And we
Only did what poetry told us to do.

The Blue Flannel Suit

I had let it all grow. I had supposed
It was all OK. Your life
Was a liner I voyaged in.
Costly education had fitted you out.
Financiers and committees and consultants
Effaced themselves in the gleam of your finish.
You trembled with the new life of those engines.

That first morning,
Before your first class at College, you sat there
Sipping coffee. Now I know, as I did not,
What eyes waited at the back of the class
To check your first professional performance
Against their expectations. What assessors
Waited to see you justify the cost
And redeem their gamble. What a furnace
Of eyes waited to prove your metal. I watched
The strange dummy stiffness, the misery,
Of your blue flannel suit, its straitjacket, ugly
Half-approximation to your idea
Of the proprieties you hoped to ease into,
And your horror in it. And the tanned
Almost green undertinge of your face
Shrunk to its wick, your scar lumpish, your plaited
Head pathetically tiny.
                              You waited,
Knowing yourself helpless in the tweezers
Of the life that judged you, and I saw
The flayed nerve, the unhealable face-wound
Which was all you had for courage.
I saw that what gripped you, as you sipped,
Were terrors that had killed you once already.
Now, I see, I saw, sitting, the lonely

Girl who was going to die.
                              That blue suit.
A mad, execution uniform,
Survived your sentence. But then I sat, stilled,
Unable to fathom what stilled you
As I looked at you, as I am stilled
Permanently now, permanently
Bending so briefly at your open coffin.

Daffodils

Remember how we picked the daffodils?
Nobody else remembers, but I remember.
Your daughter came with her armfuls, eager and happy,
Helping the harvest. She has forgotten.
She cannot even remember you. And we sold them.
It sounds like sacrilege, but we sold them.
Were we so poor? Old Stoneman, the grocer,
Boss-eyed, his blood-pressure purpling to beetroot
(It was his last chance,
He would die in the same great freeze as you),
He persuaded us. Every Spring
He always bought them, sevenpence a dozen,
'A custom of the house'.

Besides, we still weren't sure we wanted to own
Anything. Mainly we were hungry
To convert everything to profit.
Still nomads – still strangers
To our whole possession. The daffodils
Were incidental gilding of the deeds,
Treasure trove. They simply came,
And they kept on coming.
As if not from the sod but falling from heaven.
Our lives were still a raid on our own good luck.
We knew we'd live for ever. We had not learned
What a fleeting glance of the everlasting
Daffodils are. Never identified
The nuptial flight of the rarest ephemera –
Our own days!
                    We thought they were a windfall.
Never guessed they were a last blessing.
So we sold them. We worked at selling them
As if employed on somebody else's

Flower-farm. You bent at it
In the rain of that April – your last April.
We bent there together, among the soft shrieks
Of their jostled stems, the wet shocks shaken
Of their girlish dance-frocks –
Fresh-opened dragonflies, wet and flimsy,
Opened too early.

We piled their frailty lights on a carpenter's bench,
Distributed leaves among the dozens –
Buckling blade-leaves, limber, groping for air, zinc-
    silvered –
Propped their raw butts in bucket water,
Their oval, meaty butts,
And sold them, sevenpence a bunch –

Wind-wounds, spasms from the dark earth,
With their odourless metals,
A flamy purification of the deep grave's stony cold
As if ice had a breath –

We sold them, to wither.
The crop thickened faster than we could thin it.
Finally, we were overwhelmed
And we lost our wedding-present scissors.

Every March since they have lifted again
Out of the same bulbs, the same
Baby-cries from the thaw,
Ballerinas too early for music, shiverers
In the draughty wings of the year.
On that same groundswell of memory, fluttering
They return to forget you stooping there
Behind the rainy curtains of a dark April,
Snipping their stems.

But somewhere your scissors remember. Wherever they
    are.

Here somewhere, blades wide open,
April by April
Sinking deeper
Through the sod – an anchor, a cross of rust.

The Bee God

When you wanted bees I never dreamed
It meant your Daddy had come up out of the well.

I scoured the old hive, you painted it,
White, with crimson hearts and flowers, and bluebirds.

So you became the Abbess
In the nunnery of the bees.

But when you put on your white regalia,
Your veil, your gloves, I never guessed a wedding.

That Maytime, in the orchard, that summer,
The hot, shivering chestnuts leaned towards us.

Their great gloved hands again making their offer
I never know how to accept.

But you bowed over your bees
As you bowed over your Daddy.

Your page a dark swarm
Clinging under the lit blossom.

You and your Daddy there in the heart of it,
Weighing your slender neck.

I saw I had given you something
That had carried you off in a cloud of gutturals –

The thunderhead of your new selves
Tending your golden mane.

You did not want me to go but your bees
Had their own ideas.

You wanted the honey, you wanted those big blossoms
Clotted like first milk, and the fruit like babies.

But the bees' orders were geometric –
Your Daddy's plans were Prussian.

When the first bee touched my hair
You were peering into the cave of thunder.

That outrider tangled, struggled, stung –
Marking the target.

And I was flung like a headshot jackrabbit
Through sunlit whizzing tracers

As bees planted their volts, their thudding electrodes,
In on their target.

Your face wanted to save me
From what had been decided.

You rushed to me, your dream-time veil off,
Your ghost-proof gloves off,

But as I stood there, where I thought I was safe,
Clawing out of my hair

Sticky, disembowelled bees,
A lone bee, like a blind arrow,

Soared over the housetop and down
And locked onto my brow, calling for helpers

Who came –
Fanatics for their God, the God of the Bees,

Deaf to your pleas as the fixed stars
At the bottom of the well.

Being Christlike

You did not want to be Christlike. Though your father
Was your God and there was no other, you did not
Want to be Christlike. Though you walked
In the love of your father. Though you stared
At the stranger your mother.
What had she to do with you
But tempt you from your father?
When her great hooded eyes lowered
Their moon so close
Promising the earth you saw
Your fate and you cried
Get thee behind me. You did not
Want to be Christlike. You wanted
To be with your father
In wherever he was. And your body
Barred your passage. And your family
Who were your flesh and blood
Burdened it. And a god
That was not your father
Was a false god. But you did not
Want to be Christlike.

Red

Red was your colour.
If not red, then white. But red
Was what you wrapped around you.
Blood-red. Was it blood?
Was it red-ochre, for warming the dead?
Haematite to make immortal
The precious heirloom bones, the family bones.

When you had your way finally
Our room was red. A judgement chamber.
Shut casket for gems. The carpet of blood
Patterned with darkenings, congealments.
The curtains – ruby corduroy blood,
Sheer blood-falls from ceiling to floor.
The cushions the same. The same
Raw carmine along the window-seat.
A throbbing cell. Aztec altar – temple.

Only the bookshelves escaped into whiteness.

And outside the window
Poppies thin and wrinkle-frail
As the skin on blood,
Salvias, that your father named you after,
Like blood lobbing from a gash,
And roses, the heart's last gouts,
Catastrophic, arterial, doomed.

Your velvet long full skirt, a swathe of blood,
A lavish burgundy,
Your lips a dipped, deep crimson.

You revelled in red.
I felt it raw – like the crisp gauze edges
Of a stiffening wound. I could touch
The open vein in it, the crusted gleam.

Everything you painted you painted white
Then splashed it with roses, defeated it,
Leaned over it, dripping roses,
Weeping roses, and more roses,
Then sometimes, among them, a little bluebird.

Blue was better for you. Blue was wings.
Kingfisher blue silks from San Francisco
Folded your pregnancy
In crucible caresses.
Blue was your kindly spirit – not a ghoul
But electrified, a guardian, thoughtful.

In the pit of red
You hid from the bone-clinic whiteness.

But the jewel you lost was blue.

Snow

Snow falling. Snowflakes clung and melted
In the sparkly black fox fur of your hat.
Soft chandeliers, ghostly wreckage
Of the Moscow Opera. Flakes perching and
Losing their hold on the heather tips. An unending
Walk down the cobbled hill into the oven
Of empty fire. Among the falling
Heavens. A short walk
That could never end was
Never ending. Down, on down
Under the thick, loose flocculence
Of a life
Burning out in the air. Between char-black buildings
Converted to closed cafés and Brontë gift-shops.
Beyond them, the constellations falling
Through the Judaean thorns, into the fleeces
Of the Pennine sheep. Deepening
Over the faces of your school-friends,
Beside their snowed-under tanks, locked into the Steppe
Where the mud had frozen again
While they drank their coffee. You escaped
Deeper into the falling flakes. They were clinging
To the charcoal crimped black ponyskin
Coat you wore. Words seemed warm. They
Melted in our mouths
Whatever was trying to cling.
                              Leaning snow
Folded you under its cloak and ushered you away
Down the hill. Back to where you came from.

I watched you. Feeling the snow's touch.

Already, it was burying your footprints,
Drawing its white sheet over everything,
Closing the air behind you.

A Dove

Snaps its twig-tether – mounts –
Dream-yanked up into vacuum
Wings snickering.

Another, in a shatter, hurls dodging away up.

They career through tree-mazes –
Nearly uncontrollable love-weights.

Or now
Temple-dancers, possessed, and steered
By solemn powers
Through insane, stately convulsions.

Porpoises
Of dove-lust and blood splendour
With arcs
And plungings, and spray-slow explosions.

Now violently gone
Riding the snake of the long love-whip
Among flarings of mares and stallions

Now staying
Coiled on a bough
Bubbling molten, wobbling top-heavy
Into one and many.